KT-562-413

Contents

Introduction

How to use this book

This book has been written as a brand new text for those people who are working towards the new BTEC Introductory Certificate or Diploma in Health and Social Care. It covers the three Core units and six of the Optional units required for successful completion of this award.

The units included are:

1   Starting work in health and social care

2   Working in health and social care

3   Developing skills in health and social care

4   Personal effectiveness

5   Social responsibility at work

6   Health and the environment

7   Looking after children

8   Images of people

With each unit the text is organised under the same headings as the qualification, to make it easy for you to follow. By working through each of the units you will find the knowledge and information that you require to help you complete this award.

Special features in the book

Throughout the text there are a number of special features to encourage you to think more widely about the area of study you are engaged in. They are designed to encourage you to take part in discussions or undertake some research that is relevant to the subject matter that you are following.

● ● ● *Case studies*

These are examples of real-life situations (or simulations) involving clients in the health, social care and early years sectors. The questions or notes attached to each case study will enable you to examine key issues and deepen your understanding of the subject.

• • • *Give it a go*

Relevant health, social care and early years issues are raised for you to discuss or work through with another person or on your own.

• • • *What if ...*

These describe situations that could arise and which you might face in the health, social care and early years sectors. They offer you the opportunity for problem-solving.

• • • *Evidence activity*

These are activities that will provide you with practice evidence to show that you understand the work required in the unit. By working through the tasks as shown in the evidence activity, you will have an opportunity to obtain a pass, merit or distinction grade for that unit.

Other features included in this book are:

- A number of very helpful **website addresses**. We strongly recommend that you visit some of these as you work through your qualification.
- **Key terms** are explained as they occur within the text. You should find this helpful because the jargon (specialised language) used by health, social care and early years workers can be challenging to learn in the early stages of your study.

We are sure that you will receive excellent guidance and support from the institution where you are following your qualification. That, together with the information included in this book, should be sufficient to ensure that you have an enjoyable and informative year of study as you begin your journey towards employment in the health, social care and early years sectors.

Best wishes with your studies.

Sarah Horne
Jo Irvine
Lynda Mason

unit 1

Starting work in health and social care

In this unit you will investigate a variety of different jobs in the health, social care and early years sectors. You will begin to discover the many skills that are needed for individual jobs and find out about the training that you will need to further your career.

You will also examine the many different types of organisations in the health, social care and early years sectors. You will investigate large organisations that work across the whole country and smaller organisations that work in local communities.

The job you choose to do will have an effect on your future lifestyle. You will explore how lifestyle may influence the choices you make about your career.

In this unit you will learn about:

▷ the different types of jobs available within the health, social care and early years sectors

▷ the different types of organisation and venues in the sector

▷ the relationship between lifestyle and job choices.

Different types of jobs

Types of jobs

We will start by investigating a variety of different types of jobs.

• • • *Supervisory level jobs*

You may want a job with a lot of responsibility where you are in charge of other people. This type of job usually requires a high level of training, but as it provides higher pay many people aim to progress to this level of work.

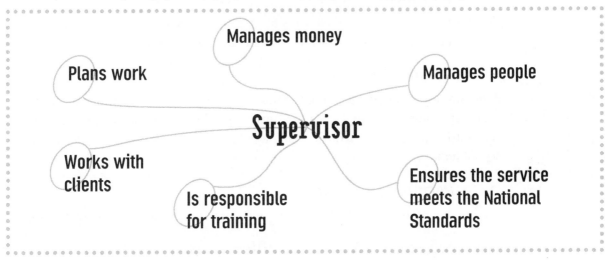

Plans work

Manages money

Manages people

Works with clients

Supervisor

Is responsible for training

Ensures the service meets the National Standards

• • • *Part-time work*

Part-time work is described as anything less than the regular number of hours worked in a week (generally 37 hours per week). It suits people who have other responsibilities in their lives such as the care of a child or elderly relative. Many people returning to work gain confidence by starting off in a part-time job.

CASE STUDY part-time job

List the advantages of having a part-time job for the following people:

▷ Sarah has two children aged 6 and 3 years. She works every morning at Merryvale Pre-school.

▷ Louise has not worked since leaving school. She has just got a job as a care assistant at Cosy Hall Nursing Home, three evenings a week. Her partner will look after the children when he gets home from work.

▷ Dan works in a school supporting a child with special needs during the day, but also has a part-time job at the out-of-school club at the local community centre.

Part-time employees now have the same rights and benefits as full-time employees. These include holiday pay, sickness benefit and access to a pension scheme.

••• *Full-time work*

Different organisations have their own descriptions of 'full-time' work and the hours of work may vary. The average number of hours each week is 37 hours. Sometimes people in a full-time job are also able to work overtime hours, or 'unsocial' hours, for which the rate of pay may be higher.

••• *Temporary work*

This term describes a job which runs for a limited period of time. Temporary staff are often employed to cover sick leave, holiday leave or maternity leave.

••• *Seasonal work*

Sometimes staff are employed for a short period of time at specific times of the year. For example, a care setting that provides holiday care may employ additional staff during the summer months. Holiday play schemes only employ staff in the school holidays.

••• *Permanent work*

A permanent job does not have a fixed end date and provides a level of security.

••• *Skilled work and unskilled work*

All people working in the health, social care and early years sectors will develop a range of skills to help them do the job. However, some jobs require additional knowledge and skills that you can get by attending a training course. Skilled jobs often provide a higher rate of pay.

SKILLED WORK
e.g. a nursery nurse who has been trained in child development.

UNSKILLED WORK
e.g. a domestic worker carrying out routine tasks.

CASE STUDY   what type of job?

Decide what type of job these people have just got:

▷ Jamilla has just got a job as a live-in carer for three weeks in August with the Seaview Trust that provides holidays for people with disabilities.

▷ Tom has just got his first regular job as a childcare professional in a new children's centre, working from 8 a.m. to 4 p.m. five days a week.

▷ Sheila has just got a job as a cleaner at Cosy Hall Care Home. She will work for four hours a day while Maria is on maternity leave.

Job titles and job roles

Where the job title includes the word 'assistant' it describes someone who works under the direction of another person. Here is a list of some of the jobs you might apply for.

HEALTH	SOCIAL CARE	EARLY YEARS
Health care assistant	Care assistant	Pre-school assistant
Dental surgery assistant	Domiciliary carer	Classroom assistant
Physiotherapy assistant		Play work assistant
Occupational therapy assistant		

Direct care

Direct carers are people who work directly with clients.

A care worker in a residential home giving an older person a drink.

A childcare worker bottle feeding a baby.

Two care workers have written you a letter describing their different job roles.

Residential care worker

I work in a Residential Home for the elderly. In the morning I help the clients get up. It was quite difficult the first time I had to dress an older person, but I have learnt how to help people be as independent as possible. I take round the tea and biscuits and talk to the clients. Yesterday, Tom was worried that his daughter could not visit him. I cheered him up by talking about all the naughty things he got up to when he was a child. After serving the dinner, I help with the painting class.

Domiciliary care worker

I am working with another domiciliary care worker. We visit a lady called Amy who is 92 and lives on her own. She broke her leg a few months ago, so cannot manage without help. We help her have a bath, do the washing for her and vacuum round the house. Then we take her for a short walk. She is very independent and does not like the fact that she can no longer walk outside on her own. The carer I work with has to check that Amy has taken her medicine because she is a bit forgetful these days.

GIVE IT A GO working with clients

List all the ways these students work directly with their clients.

Health care worker (nursing assistant)

I work on a surgical ward (for people having operations) in the local hospital. I help both the patients and the staff. I collect x-rays from the x-ray department and take blood samples to the laboratory. I often help patients unpack when they first arrive. They are often very nervous so I have to be friendly and reassuring. I help to make beds and keep the ward tidy, and arrange the patient's flowers and cards. Sometimes I fill in the menu cards when patients are choosing what they want to eat.

Childcare worker (nursery nurse)

I am on placement in a private nursery. Every morning I have to help the staff set out the toys and equipment. We have to be very careful about safety for young children. When the children arrive I talk to them while they play. Yesterday we made playdough together, which the children really enjoyed. This morning, when Farhan arrived, he did not want to leave his mummy and he was crying. I had to comfort and distract him. I managed to get him to stop crying by reading him *The Hungry Caterpillar*

GIVE IT A GO finding out about the job

Working with a friend, make a list of questions you could ask a health, social care and early years worker about his or her job. Try and find an opportunity to meet with a health, social care and early years professional and ask him or her your questions. Record the answers and place the record in your file.

Indirect care

Indirect carers provide support for those who work directly with clients. This helps the direct carers to do their jobs efficiently.

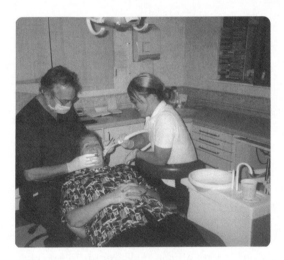

A dental nurse assists the dentist during treatment.

● ● ● *Dental nurse*

The dental nurse is responsible for sterilising the instruments and passing them to the dentist during treatment. She will prepare some of the materials the dentist uses, process x-rays and keep good records about the patients. The dental nurse will need good written skills and a good understanding of hygiene procedures.

● ● ● *Receptionist*

A client's first impressions of a service is often provided by the receptionist, so he or she should be friendly and approachable, both in person and when on the telephone. People may be very nervous when visiting health or social care settings.

● ● ● *Administrator*

An administrator may not have as much client contact as a receptionist, but should understand the needs of people who use health and social care services. This job involves keeping records, dealing with money, organising stock and planning services. The administrator will have good organisational, numeracy and IT skills.

● ● ● *Housekeeper*

The housekeeper is responsible for running a residential children's home or a care home for elderly or disabled people. She or he may arrange the cleaning and domestic affairs of the house, organise the catering, and support the care workers in their role. The housekeeper needs to be very organised and efficient, and a good time manager.

• • • *Porter*

The porter is responsible for moving patients around the hospital between wards, operating theatres, physiotherapy or x-ray. People are apprehensive in hospital and it is important that a hospital porter is friendly, approachable and reassuring. Porters also transport blood, specimens and medical equipment as required.

◼◼◼ EVIDENCE ACTIVITY

Job advertisements

Look in the local paper, job centre and the employment section of your Local Authority and NHS Trust website for jobs in the health, social care and early years sectors. Keep copies of these advertisements for your file.

You should identify the following:

▷ Is the job part-time, full-time, permanent or temporary?

▷ Is the job for a direct carer or indirect carer?

▷ Which of the positions you have found would you most like to apply for? Explain why.

Qualifications and skills

• • • *Essential and desirable requirements*

There are two parts of a job description:

1. A description of what the job involves – this lists all the tasks required by the job.

2. A person specification – this describes the type of person who is wanted in the job and the skills that he or she should have.

These skills are explained as:

- Essential requirements – the skills you must have to apply for the job.
- Desirable requirements – some of the skills you might be expected to have.

CASE STUDY   essential and desirable requirements

Read the three job descriptions below and identify the essential and desirable requirements for each job.

Health care assistant

You will assist nursing staff and provide for patient care, including feeding, hygiene and toilet needs. You will observe patients' condition and report to nursing staff. You will undertake patient moving and handling appropriately and safely, and assist patients to walk. Essential requirements include good communication skills, confidentiality and the ability to work as part of a team. At least one year's experience in a hospital or care setting would be desirable.

Playwork assistant

You will be responsible for setting up and supporting safe play experiences for children aged 5–11 years. You will attend planning meetings and support the play leaders in general administrative duties. You will sometimes act as an escort on the playscheme bus. Hours of work are 2.30–5.30 p.m. Monday to Friday. Qualifications are not essential as training will be part of the job. However, you must be hardworking and willing to learn. An interest in sport would be desirable.

Care assistant

You will support two ladies and a gentleman who live in their own home, providing help with aspects of daily living and personal care and encouraging their independence. They enjoy gardening, painting and trips to the park. You will work on a rota basis with some evening and weekend work. Punctuality, reliability and a neat and tidy appearance are essential for this post. Qualifications not essential but you will be expected to work towards an NVQ Level 2.

• • • *Pathways and career routes*

To improve your chances of getting a job, you can gain:

- a qualification
- experience.

Qualifications that you might progress towards are:

Health and Social Care

- NVQ 2 in Care
- GNVQ Foundation in Health and Social Care (Level 1)
- BTEC Introductory Certificate and Diploma in Health and Social Care (Level 1)
- GNVQ Intermediate in Health and Social Care (Level 2)
- BTEC First Certificate and Diploma in Health and Social Care (Level 2).

Childcare

- NVQ 2 in Early Years Care and Education
- Foundation Certificate in Caring for Children (Level 1)
- Certificate in Childcare and Education (Level 2).

⬚⬚⬚ EVIDENCE ACTIVITY

Qualifications and experience

Using the job advertisements gathered during the previous evidence activity, examine the qualifications and essential and desirable requirements for a range of different jobs. Identify the following:

▷ the job title

▷ the qualifications required for the job

▷ the essential requirements for the job

▷ the desirable requirements for the job.

● ● ● Formal care experience

Formal care experience is gained through paid work or attendance at a training course with work experience. While there are some jobs that do not require specific experience, all people working in this area would be expected to undertake training.

● ● ● Informal care experience

Many people have some experience of working with others which would help when first applying for a job.

Informal care experience

- Cared for an older relative
- Helped out at the Brownies
- Babysitting
- Helped a neighbour with shopping
- Cared for younger brothers or sisters
- Helped a friend with a disability

CASE STUDY informal care experience

During years 10 and 11, Caroline went to the local special school every Wednesday afternoon. Sometimes she helped the wheelchair dancing class and sometimes she helped in the music and movement class. She learnt to work as part of a team, follow instructions and communicate with children with disabilities. She became very good at steering a wheelchair and learnt how to support children sitting on the floor.

▷ How did this experience help Caroline prepare for a career in the care sector?

▷ List all the experiences you have had that might prepare you for a career in the health, social care or early years sectors.

Qualities for jobs

• • • *Age*

The Care Standards Act 2000 recommends that workers should be 18 years before gaining employment. You must be 16 years old to join a qualification childcare course and cannot be left alone with children if you are under the age of 18 years.

• • • *Legal requirements*

Jobs in the care sector are exempt from the Rehabilitation of Offenders Act 1974. This means that all people who work in the care setting must be checked by the Criminal Records Bureau to ensure that staff are safe to work with vulnerable people.

• • • *Personal qualities*

The following questionnaire has been completed to show the personal qualities needed for a job in the health, social care and early years sectors.

Question	Answer
1 Why is it important to be punctual?	If you are late you will hold up the work and the clients will suffer. Clients may need to be out of bed for breakfast so you cannot be late. A nursery cannot open unless the correct number of staff are present.
2 Why is it important to be honest?	People must be able to trust you. You may have to look after other people's possessions such as money, toiletries or cigarettes, and you must not be tempted to take them.
3 Why is it important to have a happy and friendly personality?	People who are unwell or nervous need friendly, happy and reassuring people to help them feel comfortable.
4 Why is it important to be healthy and fit?	You must be reliable and not take lots of days off sick. You must be fit to help lift people the correct way, carry things and pick up children.
5 Why is it important to be efficient and responsible, and to follow instructions?	Clients have many needs so it is important to be efficient and do what you are told quickly. If you have been asked to see that a client has a drink of water every half hour, you must see that he or she does drink – the client needs to have lots of water to keep well.
6 Why is it important to use your initiative?	You may be nervous when you first start work but you will watch other people and learn what needs to be done. Sometimes you need to use your initiative to see what needs to be done without being told.
7 Why is it important to be non-judgemental?	You will meet many people who have different views and different standards to yourself. You will work with people who are ill, have difficulties in their lives or may not be able to do what they used to do. It is most important that you are able to show respect to all people.

WHAT if

Personal qualities

...*You were the manager of a care home?*

Last night Lizzie was out on the town. She drank too much so slept in, missed her bus and was late for work. 'Where have you been,' the manager asked as she rushed through the door. 'My bus was cancelled, I had to wait for the later one.' 'Well hurry up and go and get Mrs Winter out of bed for her breakfast,' the manager said. When the manager had gone, Lizzie slipped into the kitchen, helped herself to a piece of the patients' bread, and took some of Mrs Summer's orange juice to swallow a pill for her headache. Then she went to see Mrs Winter. 'Come on, hurry up. Your breakfast is getting cold, we haven't time for a wash this morning,' Lizzie said sharply as she helped Mrs Winter out of bed.

▷ Find six mistakes that Lizzie has made this morning?

▷ Imagine you are the manager. What are you going to say to Lizzie?

Different types of organisations

You will now explore the three different ways that health, social care and early years services for people in this country are provided:

- statutory
- voluntary and charitable
- private.

These services are encouraged to work in partnership to provide a better quality of care for vulnerable people. They vary in size from large national organisations to small local ones.

Statutory services

Statutory services are services funded by the state with money provided through taxes. Details of statutory services are given in the diagram overleaf.

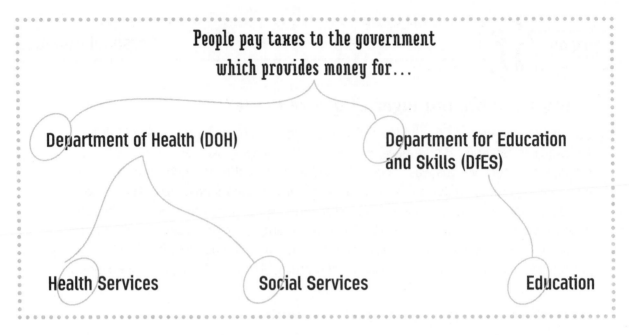

People pay taxes to the government which provides money for...
- Department of Health (DOH)
- Department for Education and Skills (DfES)
- Health Services
- Social Services
- Education

••• *The Health Service*

Following the formation of the National Health Service (NHS) in 1948, the government was committed to providing free access to health care for all people. The NHS is the largest employer in Europe. Currently, services are provided as follows:

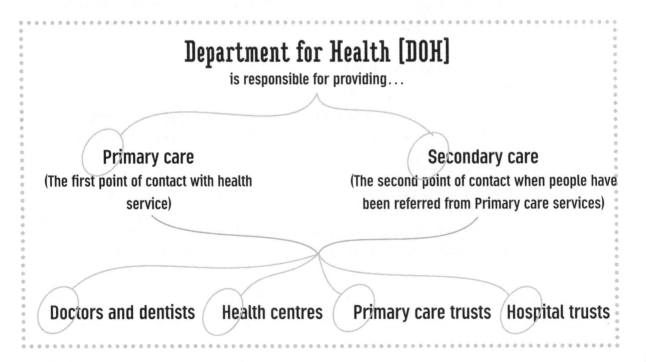

Department for Health [DOH] is responsible for providing...

- Primary care (The first point of contact with health service)
- Secondary care (The second point of contact when people have been referred from Primary care services)
- Doctors and dentists
- Health centres
- Primary care trusts
- Hospital trusts

Some doctors and dentists have their own practices or they may work in a health centre. Health centres are able to provide:

- health education – to prevent illness
- diagnosis – to identify illness
- treatment – to treat illness.

GIVE IT A GO   see what's available

In small groups, visit a local doctor's surgery or health centre to see what services are available.

◻ Collect three leaflets about health education to share with your class before putting them in to your portfolio.

◻ Compare the services provided at a doctor's surgery with the services provided at a health centre.

You might have found some of these services at your local health centre:

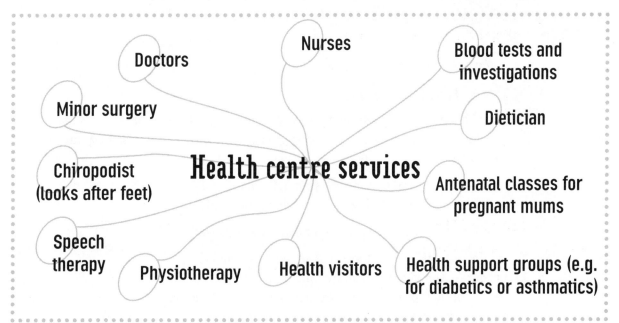

Nurses

Doctors

Blood tests and investigations

Minor surgery

Dietician

Chiropodist (looks after feet)

Health centre services

Antenatal classes for pregnant mums

Speech therapy

Physiotherapy

Health visitors

Health support groups (e.g. for diabetics or asthmatics)

CASE STUDY health centre

The receptionist at the local health centre is tidying her records before going home. This is a list of some of the people she has spoken to today.

▷ Paula is 8 years old and has just been diagnosed with diabetes. She was sent to see the diabetic nurse at the support group.

▷ Mrs Poole is 74 years old and has come to have her leg ulcer dressed. She will also see the physiotherapist to get a walking stick to help her walk.

▷ Mrs Patel has brought Farzana, who is 6 months, to see the health visitor for her development check, and Irfan to see the doctor about his bad cough.

▷ Mrs Paterson has had a blood test and went to the antenatal class.

▷ Mr Primrose had a mole on his arm removed last week. He came to see the nurse to have his stitches removed.

▷ Patrick is 5 years old. His mum was worried about his speech development so the health visitor suggested he see the speech therapist.

1 The people in each example have seen two professionals. Who are they?

2 Working with another person, discuss the advantages of having all these services in one health centre.

● ● ● *Hospital trusts*

Hospitals provide a wide range of services to diagnose (identify) illness and provide treatment and care for people who are ill. You can access hospital care in two ways:

- through referral by a health professional
- as an emergency following an accident or incident.

These are some of the services a hospital will provide:

- doctors (diagnose illness and suggest treatment)
- nurses (provide medical treatment and care)
- physiotherapists (provide exercises, chest care and help mobility)
- occupational therapists (help people with aspects of daily living)
- radiographers (people who take x-rays)
- dieticians (provide advice and support about food)
- social workers (provide social care services)
- laboratory technicians (undertake laboratory work to help diagnose illness)
- pharmacists (provide medicines)
- porters (move people and equipment from one place to another).

A physiotherapist in practice.

A laboratory assistant.

CASE STUDY) hospital services

Last July, Florence, who is 92, fell in the garden and broke her leg. The ambulance took her to the hospital's accident and emergency department. After her x-ray a porter took her to Ward 9 where the nurses made her comfortable until she had her operation. The next day the physiotherapist came and taught her some exercises for her leg. After a few days, Florence began to feel rather ill and she had a blood test. This showed that she had an infection, so the doctor prescribed some antibiotics. A physiotherapy assistant came every day to help Florence practise walking. Florence had lost a lot of weight so the dietician prescribed some nourishing drinks to help build up her strength. One day the occupational therapist took Florence to the kitchen and gave her a gadget to help her pour water from a heavy kettle. Before Florence went home, the social worker visited her to arrange for a home help. Eight weeks after her accident, Florence was very happy to be back in her own home.

How was Florence helped by all the professionals in the list above during her stay in hospital?

••• Social Services provision

Social Services provision includes:

- support for people with disabilities
- residential care for children and adults
- day care services and family centres
- a child protection service
- arrangements for fostering and adoption.

◻◻◻ EVIDENCE ACTIVITY

Social Services

Using the Internet, find out about all the services offered by Social Services in your local area. Collect any information and put it in your file.

••• Family centres

Family centres are similar to health centres in that they provide several services for children and families in the same building:

- childcare for children aged 0–5 years
- nursery education for children aged 3–5 years
- support for parents to develop parenting skills
- parent and toddler sessions
- support for families where child protection is an issue.

◻◻◻ EVIDENCE ACTIVITY

Family centre

Write to a local family centre and ask for a copy of their information leaflet to put in your file.

••• Local Education Authority provision

••• Schools

The Local Education Authority (LEA) is responsible for educational provision in any area:

- nursery schools for children aged 3–5 years
- primary schools for children aged 5–11 years
- secondary schools for children aged 11–16 years
- schools for children with specific needs.

While schools receive money from the government they are managed by a governing body, which may include teachers, a representative from the LEA and parents. The governing body makes many of the decisions about how the school is run and is responsible for appointing staff.

There are lots of different jobs that involve working with children in a school environment.

CASE STUDY working in a school

Liam has just come home from his first day at school. 'What is your teacher called?' his dad asks. Liam can't remember. During the day he met Mr Mustard the head teacher, Mrs Black his class teacher and Miss Green the classroom assistant, who put his painting on the wall. He met Miss Brown the special support assistant, who helps Jason who has cerebral palsy move around, and Mrs Grey the welfare assistant, who looked after Liam at dinner time.

1   Why do you think Liam could not remember what his teacher was called?

2   List all the different people Liam met and state what their jobs are.

• • • *Schools for children with special needs*

Some children with multiple (many) difficulties attend schools where the staff have particular training and skills, and where there is special equipment to help the children's development. However, many children with additional needs now attend mainstream (local) schools where a member of staff called a special support assistant helps them.

Voluntary and charitable provision

Voluntary and charitable groups do not make a profit. Voluntary organisations get some money to support their work by fund raising. They may also apply to government agencies, such as Social Services or the Lottery, for grants to fund specific projects. Charities and voluntary organisations were originally set up by volunteers (people who do not get paid for their work) to provide support for a particular group of people. For example, Barnardos was originally set up to provide for orphan children, and Age Concern was set up to support and publicise the needs of older people. Voluntary organisations often employ paid staff to co-ordinate their work.

CASE STUDY — Age Concern

Jessie is 81 years old. She lives on her own with five cats. One day every week she is collected in a minibus and taken to the Age Concern day centre. She has a bath and her hair is washed, then she eats a cooked dinner. In the afternoon, Jessie uses a computer to write the story of her childhood to send to her grandchildren.

▢ Many Age Concern projects provide day centres like the one Jessie visits. Visit the Age Concern website (www.ageconcern.org.uk) to find out more.

▢ Why does Jessie like visiting the day centre?

WHAT if

...you were a volunteer with Age Concern?

Choose one task you would like to do and describe why you would do it well:

▢ help in one of the charity shops, sorting donations and serving the public

▢ help in a day centre

▢ be an escort on the mini-bus

▢ visit people living alone at home and carry out simple errands like shopping, small repairs or gardening duties

▢ get involved in fundraising events

▢ help with a computer class.

You may have identified a skill that will help you to get a paid job.

● ● ● *National Society for the Prevention of Cruelty to Children (NSPCC) (www.nspcc.org.uk)*

The NSPCC is an organisation which helps to protect children from abuse. Some of its work includes:

- supporting children and families
- investigating child protection situations
- running a child protection helpline
- providing child protection training
- providing public education
- fundraising.

• • • *Barnardos (www.barnardos.org.uk)*

Barnardos is the largest children's charity in Britain. It works with vulnerable children, young people and communities, and aims to give all children the best possible chance in life. (Note: Barnardos has a special site for student projects.)

CASE STUDY voluntary services

I want to tell you about our Breakfast Club. Julie started it three years ago because lots of the local children did not get breakfast before going to school. I was one of the first volunteers. It really suited me as I could take my son with me every day. We were a small group of young mums and enjoyed the work so much that Julie arranged for a teacher from college to run an NVQ Level 2 course just for us. We had our lessons round the table in the meeting room. Our assessor came regularly to watch us working and at the end of the year we all passed. My friends have got jobs in other places but now I am employed at the Breakfast and Out-of-School Club.

▷ What are the advantages of a Breakfast Club for the parents and children in this community?

▷ How could volunteering help you to get a job?

• • • *National Children's Home (NCH) (www.nch.org.uk)*

The National Children's Home works to improve the lives of vulnerable children and young people. It offers lots of different services to meet the needs of local people.

Services for children at risk include:

- schools for children with special educational needs
- family centres to help where there is a child protection concern
- foster care and adoption services.

Services for families include:

- family and community centres
- projects for young carers
- support for divorced or separating parents.

Services for vulnerable young people include:

- help for young people leaving care
- young homeless people projects
- projects to prevent truancy.

• • • Leonard Cheshire (www.leonard-cheshire.org.uk)

The Leonard Cheshire Foundation is the leading charity providing services for disabled people in Britain. The main aim is to help people with disabilities to live independent lives. The charity provides care for people in residential homes, day centres and for people living at home. One project involves providing computer equipment to young disabled people to help them develop the skills to find a job.

• • • Young Minds (www.youngminds.org.uk)

Young Minds is a national charity which works to improve the mental health of all children and young people by helping children to feel good about themselves. It provides several different services:

- confidential information for parents
- support for children with mental health problems
- booklets, leaflets and magazines
- training
- research.

■■■ EVIDENCE ACTIVITY

Voluntary organisations

Working with a friend, research a voluntary organisation that you would like to work for. Share your information with the rest of your class before putting it in your portfolio. You can find out the following:

▢ how the organisation started

▢ what it does

▢ how volunteers help.

These are some other voluntary organisations you might like to investigate:

- www.shelter.org.uk
- www.helptheaged.org.uk
- www.the-childrens-society.org.uk

Private organisations

A private organisation is one that works to make a profit. The organisation charges fees directly to the client and uses the money gained to provide the services. For example, Naomi's family pay £90 each week for Naomi to be looked after in a local private nursery.

• • • *Dental surgeries*

Some dental care is provided by the NHS, but currently many dentists work in private practices. Private dentists charge a higher fee for their services than NHS dentists charge.

• • • *Opticians*

People pay to visit the optician and have a sight test. Regular sight tests are particularly important for both young children and the elderly, in order to detect conditions such as diabetes, glaucoma or high blood pressure. People over the age of 60 are entitled to free eye tests; the optician can claim back the costs of these tests from the NHS.

• • • *Residential care homes*

Many residential care homes are provided by private companies. They cater for frail elderly people and people with disabilities. The owner or manager is responsible for making sure that the home meets the National Care Standards.

• • • *Special needs care homes*

People with special needs often live in small community-based or family homes. Clients often go out to day centres or the local college.

• • • *Nurseries*

Private nurseries provide care and education for children from birth to 5 years. The owner or manager is responsible for the setting. Children can attend full-time or part-time while their parents are at work. Many nurseries have different rooms for children of different ages. Some companies run their own nurseries for the children of their employees.

• • • *Pre-schools*

Pre-schools look after children aged 2 and a half to 5 years, and provide care for 2.5 to 4 hours each day. Some pre-schools are run as private businesses, with an owner or manager who is responsible for the provision.

• • • *Out-of-school clubs*

Out-of-school clubs provide for children before and after school, and usually cater for children aged 5–11 years. Most out-of-school clubs also run holiday clubs.

⬛⬛⬛ EVIDENCE ACTIVITY

Job search

This activity will help you apply for a job.

▷ Find the address and telephone number of local examples of all the private businesses described above. You can use a directory, such as the *Yellow Pages*, to help you.

▷ Choose one organisation and describe why you would like to work there and what type of job you could do in that organisation.

Size of organisations

Care services in this country are provided by large national organisations and small independent or local ones. You may feel more comfortable in a small organisation or you may like the challenge of working in a large one.

● ● ● *Small businesses*

There are many small private businesses running residential care homes or nurseries. A small private home for people with learning difficulties may have an owner and one or two members of staff. A childminder probably works alone and runs his or her own business.

● ● ● *Large privately-owned organisations*

There are many large organisations which provide care homes or nurseries all over the country, for example, BUPA (www.bupa.co.uk).

Statutory provision, e.g. Social Services care home

Large private company with care homes or nurseries in different towns

Residential care service or nursery provision

National voluntary charitable organisation

Small private company

BUPA is an international health and care organisation, which works in nearly 190 countries. It provides private medical insurance, hospitals, health assessments, care homes and childcare provision all round the country. You can use the Internet to learn more about BUPA.

The chart on page 28 demonstrates how services for the elderly or young children can be provided by both large national or small independent organisations.

• • • *Partnership*

The government is keen to encourage statutory, private and voluntary services to work in partnership to provide services for the community. In relation to work with children and young people, professionals will be encouraged to work together in multidisciplinary teams which will be based in Children's Centres.

CASE STUDY | partnerships

Merryvale Nursery School is run by the local education department. The head teacher has organised a group of childminders to look after some of the children before and after nursery, and a voluntary parent and toddler group use the main hall on Thursday afternoon.

▢ Identify examples of private, statutory and voluntary sector provision.

▢ Identify a large and small organisation.

▢ Find out if you have a new Children's Centre in your area and ask about the service it provides.

Lifestyle and job choices

Lifestyle

The term 'lifestyle' describes what we think and do, the possessions we have and the way we live. It describes the things that are important to us in the way we live our lives. It may seem that people can choose the lifestyle they lead, i.e. where to live, what to eat, or whether to smoke or take drugs. In reality, people are not always free to make these choices. Many of the factors that affect lifestyle are linked to the amount of money we have and the expectations we grow up with.

• • • *The effect of lifestyle on job choices*

Some of the factors that affect lifestyle and which may influence job choices are:

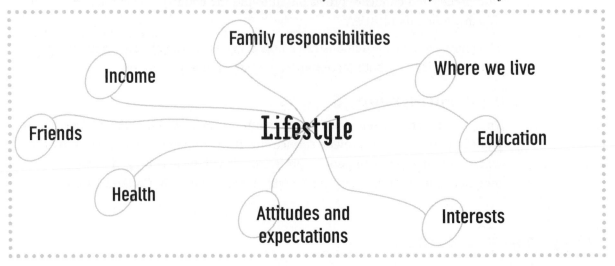

• • • *Income*

Many people want a job where they can earn lots of money. In general, these jobs carry most responsibility and generally require a high level of training. Full-time jobs usually provide more money than part-time jobs, although some people have more than one part-time job.

• • • *Family circumstances*

People who look after elderly or disabled relatives may not be free to go to work. Having children may affect they type of job you have. Some mothers choose to stay at home with their children while others only work while their children are at school.

• • • *Flexibility of location*

Where you live may affect the type of job that you do. You may want a job that is close to home so that you do not have to spend money on bus or train fares. If you have access to a car, you may be able to travel to more places for work. People living in the countryside may have a limited choice of jobs.

• • • *Social aspirations*

Social contact is a very important part of our lives. If going out in the evenings is an important part of your life, you may not want to work in the evenings. You may want a job where you can meet lots of other people with similar interests.

• • • *Health*

Some health difficulties may affect the types of job we have. A job where you have to be on your feet all day may by difficult for someone with a bad back. A person with poor health may prefer to have a part-time position.

• • • *Education*

The level of qualification will affect the type of job role that you can apply for. For many people, completing a course is a passport to a more successful career. Some people who missed out on education or had a bad experience of school may leave school with poor reading, writing and numerical skills. This may make them feel that they are unable to apply for certain jobs.

• • • *Hobbies and interests*

GIVE IT A GO hobbies and interests

Make a list of all your hobbies and interests. Have they affected your choice of course?

• • • *Attitudes and expectations*

The attitudes and expectations of your family and friends may affect your choice of career. People who grow up in homes where no one works or whose friends do not work may consider a job to be unimportant.

WHAT if   **Expectations**

...You were asked to suggest suitable jobs for these people?

▷ Richard has been working in a care home for four years and has been going to college to develop his skills. He has lots of friends, has just bought a very expensive new house, and likes responsibility.

▷ Kirsten has just moved into a small house in a new town. Most of the neighbours are elderly. She is very lonely. Her eldest child has just started school and her youngest child is going to pre-school next term.

▷ Karen had a baby when she was 15 years old and has never worked. She lives in a small, damp, overcrowded house with her mother and grandmother, neither of whom work. She is getting very depressed.

Should Richard, Kirsten and Karen:

(a) apply for a manager, assistant or unskilled job

(b) work full-time, part-time or in a temporary job?

• • • *Individual wants and needs*

All people have basic *needs* in order to survive. These include shelter, food and clothes. Everyone needs friends, love and affection. There are also many things that people *want* (e.g. mobile phones or holidays). These things will change at different stages in life.

GIVE IT A GO **individual needs**

 List all the things that are important to you at this stage in your life. This may include going out at night with your friends, having the latest mobile phone or passing your exams.

List some things you think your parents or grandparents might need.

• • • *Limitations of working hours*

Some mothers with young children may only be free to work part-time. Currently in Britain, about 5 million women have part-time jobs and approximately half of these women have young children. In other families, one partner may work a night shift so that he or she can take turns looking after children.

• • • *Personal relationships*

Once people settle in a relationship, they will be making joint decisions about their working lives.

WHAT if   **Personal relationships**

...*You had to decide what these couples should do?*

Jason and Annelise both work in a nursery in Merryvale. Annelise has just been offered a job as a manager in a nursery forty miles away.

Pearl and Adam have just bought a new house with a large mortgage. Pearl earns more money than Adam. Pearl has just discovered that she is pregnant.

What do you think each couple will do?

How will the changes affect their lifestyle?

• • • *Reasons for being at work*

Why do people go to work? Is it:

- to earn money
- to meet people and make friends
- to feel good about doing their job well?

In the care sector, people get great satisfaction and achievement from working with and supporting other people at difficult times in their lives.

GIVE IT A GO reasons for working

List all the reasons why you want a job in the care sector.

Job choices

• • • *Effect of job choice on lifestyle*

A job can take up the greater part of the day. For this reason it is important that the job you choose fits the lifestyle you prefer.

• • • *Need to earn a living*

People need money for:

- basic needs such as housing, food and clothes
- aids and gadgets to make life easier such as fridges, washing machines, cars
- entertainment such as televisions, cinema trips, going out to pubs and restaurants
- luxuries such as holidays and foreign travel.

The more money you earn, the more of these things you can have. However, the jobs that provide the most money are often those with the most responsibility and that require the most training.

• • • *Shift work*

While many jobs run from 9–5 p.m., people do not stop needing care at 5 p.m., so staff are required all through the day and night. Shift work may include morning, afternoon, evening or night shifts. These may be regular times or change every week. Often people who work night shifts have a higher rate of pay, although the hours are longer. Shift work may involve working five nights in a row and then having four days off, during which time you can go shopping, meet friends and have short holidays.

Shift work

...*You were asked why Lorraine and Dan have a problem?*

▷ Lorraine used to have an evening job at a local care home while her husband put the children to bed. Last month her marriage broke up.

▷ Dan works in a nursing home on a shift rota, working from 7 a.m. to 3 p.m. or 2 p.m. to 10 p.m.. The rota changes every week so Dan does not always have the same evenings off. Dan wants to join a course at college on Tuesday evenings.

Suggest what Lorraine and Dan might do.

● ● ● *Flexitime*

Some jobs allow people to work on a flexible basis. This means that they can start or finish work a little earlier or later if they work the extra hours on a different day. For example, Joanne has arranged to work late at the nursery on Tuesday night to help at the parents open evening. She will then be able to take an afternoon off work next week.

● ● ● *Hours of work*

Your time at work depends on your other commitments. Some people want to work long days; other people like to work for only half a day. In some jobs there is the opportunity for overtime pay if you work more than the normal working hours.

● ● ● *Starting and finishing times*

You have seen that it is possible to work at all hours of the day or night, so you need to think about the practical issues of getting to work.

- Are you good at getting up in the mornings if you have gone to bed late?
- Is public transport good very early in the morning or late at night?
- Is the traffic very busy between 8–9 a.m. and 5–6 p.m.?
- Do you feel comfortable being out alone late at night?
- Do the starting and finishing times fit in with the other responsibilities in your life?

● ● ● *Stress levels*

While some stress is good for you, since it can help you to function effectively, too much stress (that you cannot control) is not. It is therefore important to choose a job that does not cause you too much stress.

GIVE IT A GO — stress at work

What are the things that will make you stressed at work?

• • • *Personal (about you) and professional (about your work) ambitions*

Spencer is lucky. He has decided that he wants to get a job as an assistant in an out-of-school club, complete his Level 2 and then Level 3 NVQ, and eventually take a degree in youth work.

Paige cannot decide what she wants to do. She thought she would like to work in a nursery, but she enjoyed her last placement in a hospital so much that she thinks she might prefer that. She knows that she wants to marry Tim and have three children.

GIVE IT A GO — ambitions

1 Decide if you are more like Spencer or Paige.

2 Make two lists of your (a) personal and (b) professional ambitions.

• • • *Personal skills and qualities*

You need to consider if your skills match the job you want to do. Doing a job that you have the correct skills for will provide great satisfaction and motivation.

GIVE IT A GO — qualities

Look at the diagram of personal qualities on page 36.

1 How many of these qualities do you have already?

2 Which ones would you like to develop?

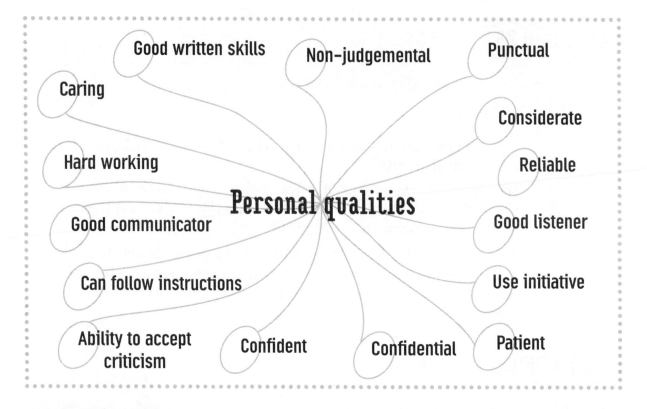

Good written skills · Non-judgemental · Punctual · Caring · Considerate · Reliable · Hard working · **Personal qualities** · Good communicator · Good listener · Can follow instructions · Use initiative · Ability to accept criticism · Confident · Confidential · Patient

GIVE IT A GO   listening

Ask a friend to read you a section from this book. When he or she has finished, ask yourself:

▭ Did you listen all the way through?

▭ Did your mind wander to other things?

▭ Can you summarise what was read?

▭ How did your friend know you were listening?

• • • *Dealing with the public*

Many of the skills described in the diagram above are needed when you work with other people. Working with the public may be very different from spending time with your friends. People may:

- be different ages (younger or much older)
- have different attitudes
- like different things
- be rude to you.

You need to consider how you will cope in different situations.

...You could choose your companion?

You have been asked to choose who you would like to accompany you on the Cosyland Care Home trip to Blackpool.

▢ Alice is a very sociable old lady who likes to talk about her family and her past. She always says thank you and is very grateful for all your help.

▢ Gertrude finds it very difficult to hear. She is often uncomfortable so she shouts a lot and can sometimes be quite rude when you try to help her.

Discuss your answer in pairs. How would you cope if you were asked to work with Gertrude?

• • • Professional qualifications

You can specialise in the following areas of work:

- care
- health care
- early years care and education (for people working with children aged 0–8 years in nurseries or pre-schools, and childminders)
- caring for children and young people (for people in residential children's homes or foster carers)
- playwork (for people working with children aged 5–15 years in out-of-school clubs and holiday play schemes).

• • • Qualification levels

There are four main levels of qualification. These are some of the qualifications at different levels:

NVQ 1	BTEC Foundation	For support staff
NVQ 2	BTEC First in Caring, GNVQ Intermediate	For assistants
NVQ 3	BTEC National Diploma, GNVQ Advanced	For supervisory roles
NVQ 4	BTEC Higher National Diploma	For managers

There is a good route for progression for people who want to develop their knowledge and skills, and gain the jobs with more responsibility and higher pay.

● ● ● *Physical and other limitations.*

All care settings are required to have an equal opportunity policy. This policy covers many aspects of work (see pages 151–153), including the employment of staff. Physical difficulties, poor eyesight and state of health should not be a barrier to work. Anyone who wants to work and can carry out the tasks listed in the job description can apply for the job. If a person's state of health makes it difficult for them to work on a full-time basis, there should be opportunities for part-time work.

Looking ahead

This unit has introduced some of the working environments and types of jobs that you may look for. By the time you have finished this course, you should be able to make a good decision about your choice of career.

 **EVIDENCE ACTIVITY**

Lifestyle factors and caring jobs

This exercise will help you to identify some of the things that are really important to you at this stage of your life.

▷ Draw a ladder with ten steps on the left-hand side of a piece of paper. Number the steps from 1 to 10, with 10 at the top.

▷ Read the following list and decide how important each factor is to you on a scale of 1 to 10.

Money ● responsibility ● meeting people ● training ● full-time work ● part-time work ● having no stress ● caring for older people ● caring for people with disabilities ● caring for children ● getting to work on time ● health ● job location ● long holidays.

▷ When you have made a decision about a factor and given it a rating between 1 and 10, place it at the appropriate step on the ladder.

When you have finished, you will see that all the things that are important to you are at the top of the ladder. Keep this exercise in your file. You can complete it again at the end of the course to see if your ideas have changed.

unit 2

Working in health and social care

This unit is designed to help you find out more about being employed in the caring services. It explains the different kinds of employment that are available, as well as the different payment methods for the work you do. The benefits of being employed in the care services are also explored, including holiday entitlements, pension rights, health schemes and other benefits.

This unit also allows you to find out more about what happens when you start work, for example, what is 'induction' and what takes place during this period? How will your performance be monitored and who does it? These and similar questions are answered as you work through this unit.

In this unit you will learn about:

▷ the terms and conditions of employment
▷ the induction and training process
▷ the procedures used to monitor performance.

Before you start

Before you can start to explore some of the main issues relating to being employed in the care services, you need to know what those main services are.

GIVE IT A GO care services

Think about all the care services that you or members of your family have used from the time you were born until now. List as many as you can.

Starting from when you were a baby, your list might include: the doctor, the health clinic, play school, nursery school, infant school, primary and secondary schools, and college. Services your parents and grandparents might have used could include:

- hospitals
- care homes
- day care.

- dental surgeries
- opticians

So, when we are talking about being employed in the care services, you can see that there is a whole range of different organisations and agencies to choose from.

Terms and conditions of employment

'Terms and conditions' is the phrase used to explain all the different aspects of being in paid employment. The terms and conditions tell us what we can expect whilst we are employed by a particular organisation or company. In the terms and conditions we would expect to see written information about:

- our employment
- our pay
- our work patterns

- our holiday entitlement
- company practices
- company benefits

Each of these aspects is now explored further.

Employment

It is useful to know that the definition of an employee states that employees:

- have fixed hours of work
- are paid a fixed wage for those hours
- are told exactly what they have to do and when they have to do it
- must have tax and insurance taken out of their wages by the employer
- can lose their job if they do not follow the rules.

An employee is often only employed by one employer at a time. However, it is possible to be employed in many different ways. For example, you could be employed full-time: this usually means working about 37 hours a week for one employer, but sometimes a little more and sometimes a little less depending on your job role. You could also be employed part-time, which means working less than full-time hours and could mean working for more than one employer at a time.

No matter what your employment hours are, you are still entitled to certain information.

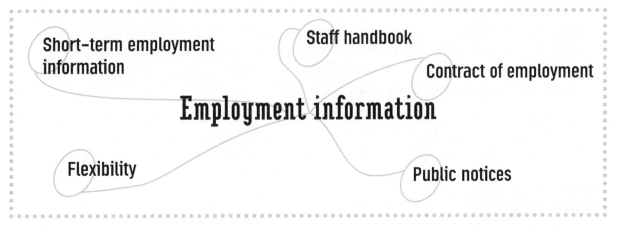

Some of these entitlements are easier to understand than others are.

• • • *Contract of employment*

This is also known as the *contract of service*. You will only receive a written contract of employment once you have been for an interview, been offered the job, and said 'yes' to the job being offered to you (a verbal agreement).

A contract of employment generally contains the following information:

- the name of the employer and the employee's name
- the date when employment began (or is due to begin)
- the rates of pay
- the hours the employee is expected to work
- holiday entitlements and holiday pay
- the place of work
- the work the employee is expected to carry out
- details of any pension schemes
- sickness entitlement (number of paid days off work with illness)
- notice requirements (if the employee wants to leave)
- disciplinary rules
- grievance procedures.

CASE STUDY | terms and conditions

Janet has been offered a new job with an early years nursery. Her terms and conditions were sent to her after she had said 'yes' to the job being offered to her. Now she has to decide whether to sign her contract of employment. In the contract, it says who she is working for and how much she will be paid. She notices that she will also be given 20 days' holiday each year plus 10 bank holidays. She is also expected to work flexibly and cover some evenings and weekends.

Janet has just noticed that she will be expected to work in two different places. On a Monday and Thursday she will be in the main nursery, but on other days she will be expected to work in a church hall close by, providing crèche services to Sure Start. 'I wonder if I will be paid travelling expenses', she thought? 'There is too much to read just now so I will have another look at it later.'

▷ Working with another student, make a list of the information that has been included in Janet's contract of employment.

GIVE IT A GO | contract of employment

Working in a group, select one of the headings to be found in a contract of employment and find out more about the regulations surrounding it. Make notes of your findings then share the information with your colleagues.

◼◼◼ EVIDENCE ACTIVITY

Working terms and conditions

1 Working with your colleagues, collect a range of job descriptions and terms and conditions for each of the following jobs:

▷ an early years worker

▷ a social carer

▷ a health worker.

2 Then, working on your own, choose two of the jobs that interest you the most. Read the job descriptions carefully and pay particular attention to the terms and conditions attached to each. Make a poster of the terms and conditions that apply to each of the jobs.

3 Finally, give a short presentation to your colleagues comparing the terms and conditions for the two jobs you have chosen.

As you can see, the contract of employment is a very important document and should be stored safely. If you do not understand any part of it you should always ask that it is explained to you.

• • • *Staff handbook*

The staff handbook is another essential document in the workplace; every workplace has to have one. You should make sure that you understand its contents and how they relate to your work. When a care service is visited by inspectors they always ask to see the staff handbook so they can check its contents.

Each handbook is likely to be different across a range of organisations but they generally contain the same kind of information. For example:

- information about the company
- health and safety regulations
- company mission statement, values and objectives
- staff contacts, roles and responsibilities
- company policies and procedures on, for example, confidentiality, data protection, appraisal
- details of client and customer rights.

GIVE IT A GO   staff handbook

Get a copy of a staff handbook from an organisation that you know. Perhaps the place where you are studying has one, or maybe you are already working and have one of your own. Have a look at the information in the handbook and then make a poster to explain the purpose of a staff handbook.

• • • *Public notices*

Some organisations have a duty to inform the public of their activities; a good example is the National Health Service (NHS). The NHS places public notices in the local press informing the population of their meetings and intended actions. This encourages individuals to attend these meetings to find out more and make their views known. Other public notices can include information relating to job vacancies or the main role and activities of organisations.

• • • *Flexibility*

Most organisations in the care sector require a certain amount of flexibility from the people who work for them. Sometimes, you are needed to work extra hours at very short notice or asked to change the work hours that you have already planned and agreed. This is very often the case when you work with vulnerable people whose care needs can change from day to day.

CASE STUDY — a change of plan

Ahmed works in a care home for older people who need additional support. He has been on duty since 1 p.m., when he cleared away the last traces of lunch. He then spent the afternoon organising and running some of the games that the residents wanted to play. They have spent time reminiscing about the past and the people they knew. Ahmed should have been finishing his shift at 8.00 p.m. but one of the night staff has called in sick. He has agreed to do a 'sleep over' in case he is needed during the night.

▷ How would you feel if you were carrying out Ahmed's job? What would you need to do to prepare for the extra hours?

Whilst these kind of changes can be irritating, especially if you had already made plans for the evening, it is important to remember that this kind of change happens all the time. If you cannot be flexible with your work time, you will need to think about taking a job that has steady hours.

GIVE IT A GO — a flexible attitude

Have a look at some job adverts for posts in the caring services, to see if any have steady hours. Which jobs ask for a flexible attitude towards working hours? Make notes of your findings. They may help you to decide at a later date which kind of job best suits your needs.

••• Short-term employment patterns

Employment on short-term, or fixed-term, contracts is increasingly available. These contracts mean that you agree to work for an employer for a specified length of time: the start and finish dates will be shown in your contract of employment. One of the reasons for an increase in the number of short-term contracts is the current funding system. Many care organisations use European funding to help with a wide range of developments, but this is often only available for short periods of time.

CASE STUDY — extra funding leads to jobs

Alice has been told that the bid she put in to the European Social Fund has been successful. This means that her organisation has been granted the money to pay for two additional members of staff for two years, to help set up a respite unit for the parents of children who have learning difficulties. Some of the funding granted can also be used to buy furniture and equipment for the new unit, which is being built at the back of the existing centre.

Alice is delighted. Now she can advertise the two posts on a short-term contract for two years.

In the previous Case Study, it is clear that the benefits of funding will help the organisation to set up a new service for its clients. There are also benefits to employees on a short-term contract. For example, employees:

- can try out new work
- can try out the organisation (see whether they like working there)
- are able to learn new skills whilst trying to find permanent work
- might be offered permanent work by the employing organisation at the end of the contract
- can move from job to job developing new skills and learning new information.

However, working short-term contracts does not suit everyone. Some people like to know where they stand and plan ahead. For these people there are disadvantages to short-term contracts. For example, employees:

- find it difficult to get a mortgage or loan
- are always having to look for new work
- may have to consider working away from home
- may have to consider not having a permanent home base.

Pay

Some people would argue that pay is the most important part of work, while others would say that 'job satisfaction' is more important. However, both are important, and you definitely need to know about the different pay methods in operation.

• • • *Hourly pay*

Most pay is worked out 'per hour'. This means that you can earn a set amount for every full hour that you work. This set amount is then multiplied by the number of hours you have worked over a period of time. For example, if you earn £5.00 per hour you would be paid the following amounts:

1 hour's work = £5.00
2 hours' work = £10.00
4 hours' work = £20.00
6 hours' work = £30.00, and so on.

WHAT if

Weekly pay

...You were working for £5.00 per hour?

How much would you expect to earn if you worked 37 hours in one week?

Employers do not normally give you the money in your hand for each hour you work. They wait until you have totalled a number of hours and then pay you for the total. They may choose to pay you every week or once a month. If, however, you are casual staff, you may be paid for just one or two hours of work at a time.

• • • *Weekly pay*

Weekly pay (often called wages) is calculated by the number of hours that you have worked. This means that you can only be paid for the week before, i.e. if you get paid on a Friday it will be for the work carried out during the previous week (known as working 'a week in hand'). You would normally be paid on the same day every week, so that you and your employer know when the money has to be paid. If you are paid in cash, the employer will go to the bank and collect the money required to put into your wage packet.

• • • *Monthly pay*

Many workplaces now pay staff on a monthly basis. This is often based on calendar months or a set date each month. If you are paid in calendar months, you would expect to have your salary paid (usually) on the last day of each month. You receive the same amount of money every month, even though some months have five weeks in them, because the money paid to you is averaged out across the year.

WHAT if   **Monthly pay**

...You were paid £5.00 per hour and worked 37 hours per week?

How much would you expect to receive at the end of one month?

• • • *Salaried*

People who earn a salary are usually on a fixed *annual* amount of money. This money is divided into 12 monthly amounts and always paid on a monthly basis.

• • • *Cash*

Payment in cash can be quite difficult to arrange because someone will need to go to the bank to withdraw the money. This can mean an individual having to walk around with a great deal of money on his or her person.

• • • Bank

The most common method of payment now used is known as banker's automated clearing system (BACS). This means that your salary can be paid directly into your bank account on 'payday'. This is a safe way of paying money to an employee and you can also access the money on the same day. Banks like to use this method because they can make regular transfers easily once they are set up. You would normally have to give your bank details to your employer so that they can make the necessary arrangements.

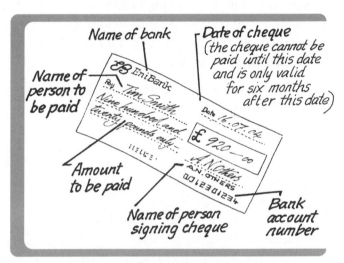

Name of bank

Date of cheque
(the cheque cannot be paid until this date and is only valid for six months after this date)

Name of person to be paid

Amount to be paid

Name of person signing cheque

Bank account number

Payment by cheque.

• • • Cheque

Some workplaces are still willing to pay their staff by cheque. However, this can be inconvenient for the individual concerned as it can take up to four or five days after putting the cheque into the bank before the money becomes available. That can be a long wait at the end of a working week or month!

Always check the information on your cheque. If it is not right, have it changed.

GIVE IT A GO   payment by cheque

Look at the cheque shown above and answer the following questions:

1   Why do you think the cheque shows the amount to be paid in writing and again in numbers?

2   Why is a signature required on the cheque?

3   How important do you think the date is?

Work patterns

In the health, social care and early years sectors there are various ways of working. Each way involves the same number of hours but they are used differently. These are called work patterns and include, for example:

- shift working
- early starts
- self-employment.
- late finishes
- flexitime

• • • *Shift working*

There are several different kinds of shift working but they all have several things in common:

- working hours that change from time to time
- working hours that can be classed as 'unsociable' (working that can stop you joining in with social activities)
- there is often a higher rate of pay for unsociable hours.

In some jobs the shift work is regular. For example, working in a factory could involve 'traditional shifts' of 6.00 a.m. to 2.00 p.m. for a week, followed by 2.00 p.m. to 10.00 p.m. for another week, and then 10 p.m. to 6.00 a.m. for a further week. Then the whole work pattern starts again.

Another pattern of working is what used to be called 'continental shifts' (now they are a common pattern of working). This involves working three 12-hour days or nights followed by four days off.

CASE STUDY | working the night shift

Irene is in bed. She came home from work at 8.00 a.m. having handed over her ward report to the day staff. She had been up all night looking after patients. She started work at 9.00 p.m. last night, had her break at 11.15 p.m. and her 'lunch' at 2.00 a.m.. She was too tired for a late meal when she got home so she just fell into bed instead. When she gets up at 6.00 p.m. she will have her breakfast. 'What an upside down way to live', she thought to herself.

D We can see that Irene is working a 'night shift' at her local hospital. However, she has started an hour earlier than other shifts often do.

Nurses often work a series of different hours referred to as earlies, lates and nights. An early shift for Irene means starting work at 7.00 a.m. and finishing at 3.00 p.m.. A late start means starting work at 3.00 p.m. and finishing at 10.00 p.m..

GIVE IT A GO | shift patterns

Working with another person, find out about the hours worked by a district nurse to see if they differ from Irene's shift patterns.

• • • *Early starts and late finishes*

For some care workers, early starts happen every few weeks. For others, early starts are a key part of the job.

When working in the care sector, staff need to be willing to change their hours at very short notice. Sometimes this can be due to an emergency with client care or another team member being off sick. In the care sector you cannot leave 'work' until another day as your clients need their care routines daily. When you are caring for people, you sometimes have to put your own needs last.

WHAT if   **Being flexible**

…You had to work extra hours?

How would you feel if you were needed in the workplace for an extra hour or two after you were supposed to have finished for the day?

• • • *Flexitime*

This is another way of organising working hours. Most people who work a flexitime system are able to start work between two set hours and finish between two or more set hours. The time spent at work each week is added up weekly. If the hours total more than the weekly amount required, then time off can be arranged. If the hours are less than the weekly amount required, more time should be spent at work in the next week, for example. People who work flexitime are usually given guidelines for when the hours to be worked can and cannot be taken.

CASE STUDY calculating flexitime

Catherine is an office administrator in a nursing home for older people. She is starting work at 9.30 a.m. today and working through until 6.30 p.m.. She has one hour for lunch. This means that she will work eight hours today. She plans to do the same for the next four days. This means that she will have worked 40 hours this week instead of the usual 37 hours. If she does the same again next week, she can save another 3 hours. Then she plans to use the 6 hours saved for a day off at the end of the month.

CASE STUDY | calculating flexitime continued

Look at the flexitime sheet that Catherine has to fill in each day:

W/C 7th Jan	In	Out	In	Out	W/C 14th Jan	In	Out	In	Out
M	8.45	12	12.30	4.00	M				
T	8.30	12	12.30	5.00	T				
W	9.30	12	12.30	4.45	W				
T	9.00	12	12.30	9.00	T				
F	8.30	12	12.30	4.00	F				
Carried forward = 0 Hours worked = 40 Total credit/owing = 3 credit					Carried forward = 3 Hours worked = Total credit/owing =				

D Working with another person, fill in a working day to suit your needs for each day of the week (don't forget to leave the lunch break) and then add your hours worked to Catherine's total to see what has happened to the hours by the end of week 2.

• • • *Days in / off*

In general, you are expected to be in work on the days that you have agreed with your manager. These are normally shown in your contract of employment. However, you can (and probably will) work other days for which you can be paid.

For some people, a 'day in' might include a Sunday. When this happens, a 'day off' is usually taken during the week. Days in and days off have to be agreed with your management. You would not normally choose them yourself, as they need to fit in with other people's working hours.

Self-employed

Self-employed people are those who work by themselves. They often have their own tools and are hired by an employer only to carry out a specific job; when the job is finished, they go and work for someone else. Self-employed people have to pay their own tax and insurance, and organise their own working day.

In care, we are likely to find that a self-employed person is one who provides a 'consultancy service'. This could be:

- carrying out research
- organising a new service
- developing new materials for use in the education of children or others.

Some self-employed people join an agency so that employers can gain access to their skills more easily.

Holiday entitlement

• • • *Annual leave*

All employed people are entitled to time off for holiday. The time off allowed is a minimum of four weeks (including statutory bank holidays). This time off has to be paid as though the employee had still worked the time expected. For example, many jobs based in the health, social care and early years sectors give a minimum of 20 holiday days per year *plus* the statutory bank holidays. Bank holidays can add as many as ten days off in a year, so for some people, 30 days' holiday a year are allowed. In addition, the number of days' holiday allowed in a year sometimes increases with the number of years' service the employee has worked.

CASE STUDY) holiday entitlement

Shanaz works for Moot House Care Home. She loves her job and has worked there for five years. She usually has 20 days' leave a year and is always very careful about planning her holidays. She likes two weeks in the summer, one week in spring and one week at Eid. She never takes a day off as holiday unless she absolutely has too. Sister Sziler, her line manager, has just told Shanaz that she will now be given an extra five days' holiday a year for long service to the company. 'Wow,' she thought, 'now I can make my summer holiday three weeks and travel further abroad if I want to'.

In pairs, discuss other ways in which Shanaz could make use of the five extra days' holiday entitlement per year. Then ask friends and relatives how many days' holiday they get each year and make a wall chart showing holiday entitlements for a range of different jobs.

• • • *Special leave*

People sometimes need special leave for a variety of reasons. For example, the death of a relative, graduation ceremonies, court appearances or jury service.

WHAT **if**   Requesting special leave

...you needed to ask for special leave?

Make a note of the circumstances that might arise in which you had to ask for special leave.

As the name suggests, special leave is 'special' and the employee must therefore ask permission from the employer to take a day off work. This could be the whole day or a part day. In some cases it will be up to the employer to decide whether the time off will be allowed (e.g. for the death of a relative). There are often company policies that tell the employee what leave might be allowed and in what circumstances.

CASE STUDY · special leave

Sylvestor has just received a written request from Carmel on one of the company forms, asking permission for a day's leave on 19 March as her aunt has died and she would like to attend the funeral. Sylvestor signed to say she could attend the funeral but that he was only willing to authorise half pay for the day instead of full pay as he had done previously. 'This is the fifth time this year that Carmel has asked for special leave. I am beginning to wonder if she is trustworthy', he thought.

Working with another person, consider these questions:

1 How many days off under special leave has Carmel taken from the start of the year?

2 Why do you think Sylvestor is worried about the number of special days off that Carmel has requested?

3 What might his response be to another request from Carmel for special leave?

4 How do you think Carmel's colleagues might feel about the time she has taken off? How would you feel in the circumstances?

Five days' special leave in twelve weeks is rather a lot. Carmel's requests could be genuine but she has managed to add an extra week to her holiday entitlement. It is likely that Sylvestor will refuse Carmel's next application for special leave, or at least refuse to pay her for the day off.

● ● ● *Public holidays*

'Public holidays' is the term used for statutory holidays. This means that every employee is entitled to the day off or, in some cases, time off instead. In the health, social care and early years sectors you cannot simply stop providing a service on Christmas Day to those people in hospital or care homes, or those receiving domiciliary care. You have a duty to continuing caring. Therefore, a system that rewards those who work on public holidays has been developed, for example, time off on another day or, in some cases, extra pay.

● ● ● *The Working Time Regulations, 1998*

The law prevents an employer asking you to work for too long. In general, these regulations state that an employer must make sure that an employee does not work more than 48 hours in a 7-day period. However, workers can choose to opt out of this rule. There are also some jobs that are exempt from this rule and there are ways of allowing staff to work longer hours.

GIVE IT A GO   Working Time Regulations

Have a look on the Internet for more information about the Working Time Regulations. Make notes of your findings and then compare them with another student's.

• • • *Time out of work*

Time out also comes under the Working Time Regulations, 1998, and covers the times we are allowed to have a break. For example:

- there should be a 20-minute rest period when the working day is longer than six hours
- there should be one day off in every seven days
- night workers should only work a maximum of eight hours
- free health assessments should be available for night workers
- adolescents should have longer rest periods and breaks than adult workers.

Again, there are more rules and regulations attached to time out and you might like to find out about these on the Internet. These rules are enforceable. This means that an employer can be made to follow the law unless the business is exempt. It is the Health and Safety Executive that make sure that all employers follow the law.

Company practices and benefits

There are a variety of different practices that can be available to us in health, social care and early years. These are sometimes seen as the benefits of working in the job and include pension rights, health schemes, and health and safety provision.

• • • *Pension rights*

A pension scheme is a way of saving up for when you retire. A small amount of money is taken from your wage each week and put into a special savings scheme. Every employee has to pay into the National Insurance Scheme by law, which means that you will have an old age pension when you retire (as well as access to health care all your life). A pension right is an additional pension which is related to the job you do. Not all companies offer pension rights but many in the health, social care and early years sectors do.

CASE STUDY) deductions from pay

'Oh no, look how much money has been taken out of my salary again this month!' thought Sarah. When she looked at her wage slip she could see that £76.00 had been taken out for her National Insurance contributions and a further £54.00 had been taken out for her company pension. 'I am only 24 years old', she thought, 'I would rather have the money now than when I am old!'

▷ What are the benefits of having an additional pension when you retire from work?

• • • *Health schemes*

Health schemes are a service offered by many companies in all types of jobs. A health scheme is a way of gaining healthcare for you and your family on a 'private' basis. Some companies offer a scheme that covers all the costs of any healthcare without taking a payment from your wage packet each month. However, this kind of scheme is becoming less popular because it costs employers too much money.

The most common kind of health scheme at present is one in which the employer makes a special deal with an insurance company to provide healthcare for their employees at a lower premium. Employees have to pay if they want to belong to the scheme.

• • • *Health and safety*

Health and safety is very important in all health, social care and early years settings, not only for the safety of clients but also for your colleagues and yourself. Every year thousands of people are injured at work. Sometimes it is because they have been careless or because they have not followed the health and safety rules that apply to their care setting. Injuries can also arise because equipment is broken or faulty, or not suitable for the job being carried out.

Health, social care and early years settings have the potential to be dangerous places in which to live or work. This is due to a variety of reasons, such as:

- many people living together (e.g. residential care)
- sick and infectious people in the same place (e.g. hospitals)
- the storage of medicines, drugs and other hazardous substances
- the use of complicated equipment for moving, handling and treating people
- the possibility of fire.

When accidents or hazardous situations occur it is usually because of a combination of one or two factors:

- human factors (actions caused or carried out by people)
- environmental factors (caused by buildings, equipment materials and substances).

The Health and Safety at Work Act 1974 is designed to protect employees in the workplace from unsafe practices. The Act is designed to:

- ensure the safety and health of workers
- protect people using the workplace (e.g. clients and service users)
- control the use of dangerous substances (e.g. medication and cleaning fluids).

This means that employers have a general duty to:

'Ensure so far as reasonably practicable the health and safety and welfare at work of all their employees.'

Employers must therefore:

- make sure that all equipment and materials are safe to use
- provide health and safety training for everyone
- make arrangements for the safe storage and handling of dangerous substances
- provide a safe place of work with safe entrances and exits.

When you begin a new job the employer must provide you with a written health and safety policy or at least make sure that you receive appropriate training for the working environment.

It is important to understand that it is not only employers who have a duty to protect the health and safety of their employees. Employees also have a general duty to:

- take reasonable care for the health and safety of themselves and others
- co-operate with the requirements and instructions provided by the employer.

Failure to carry out health and safety duties can result in accidents at work, which can in turn result in injury and death.

● ● ● *Bonuses*

CASE STUDY a Christmas bonus

Sunita has just received her December salary early. She has been paid on the 23rd of the month instead of the last day of the month. This is so she will have her salary to spend in good time for Christmas (as well as the fact that banks are closed over the festive period). She has just realised that there is an extra £50 in her wage, 'with all good wishes and thanks for your hard work this year' from Dr Halliday (home owner). Sunita thinks to herself, 'What a kind gesture'.

▷ What do you think are the benefits to Dr Halliday of paying Sunita in this way?

A bonus is an extra payment, very often made for achieving targets or sales. Bonuses are not often paid in the health, social care and early years sectors because they do not tend to work in this way. However, some private care organisations may choose to pay their staff a bonus at special times (e.g. holidays and religious festivals).

• • • *Meals on duty*

Many care establishments provide food for their service users but this does not mean that the staff working there also get a free meal. In some places this does happen but in most care organisations employees are expected to buy their own food, especially when the funding is from the public sector. It is common to find in hospitals, for example, that the food served to staff in the canteen is subsidised (the organisation contributes to the cost of the food being provided). This means that staff working in the hospital can buy their food at a cheaper price than members of the public.

• • • *Use of facilities*

In some workplaces there may be the option to use the facilities that clients use. For example, in the leisure industry staff may be able to have a free swim or use the gym before the equipment is available to members of the public. This is less likely to happen to people working in the care sector: the only time you would want to use the facilities in a hospital would be when you are ill. However, the occupational health department can sometimes arrange for staff to be seen quickly by doctors and other professions allied to medicine, for example, physiotherapists.

• • • *Working away from home conditions*

For some people, their job may require them to be away from home for much of the time. It is rare for this to happen when working in the care sector, but it does sometimes happen.

CASE STUDY working away

Eileen is a key worker in a small core and cluster home for people with learning and physical disabilities. She has been planning a holiday wth Kenny, one of her clients, for six months now and Kenny is becoming increasingly excited.

Eileen will be away for ten days, staying in a holiday camp. Her travel has been arranged and will not cost her anything. Her accommodation and food will also be paid for. However, if she wants to buy anything whilst she is away, she will have to pay for it.

▷ Eileen will obviously be working while she is away with Kenny. Why do you think her expenses have been paid?

• • • *Season ticket loans*

Some companies and organisations buy a season ticket for their local football or rugby team games. This is then used by all the staff (often in turns) as a 'perk' of the job. In some organisations, access to the season ticket is granted for good work or achieving challenging targets. Sometimes a grateful client may provide access to their season ticket. However, in the health, social care and early years sectors this kind of perk is fairly rare. In fact, we should always be wary of accepting gifts, particularly from clients.

The different uniforms of a ward sister (right) and a nurse.

• • • *Free clothes / uniform*

For most of us working in health, social care or early years, a uniform is often provided as part of the job. In some cases the uniform can be almost nationally recognised. For example, a nurse's uniform has similar characteristics no matter where in the country you live and work.

In some jobs the kind of uniform you wear also shows other people the rank or status that you hold. If we use the nurse's uniform again as an example, we often find that 'sisters' rank is a certain colour or has epaulettes on the shoulders.

CASE STUDY   benefits of uniform

Lisa starts work in the morning for the first time. She is being employed as a nursery nurse and has already been given her uniform to wear. In the morning she arrives at work in her crisp, blue trousers and the pale blue top with the nursery logo on the front. One of the children's parents greets her, saying, 'Oh, you must be the new nursery nurse, nice to meet you.' It makes Lisa feel special. During the day Lisa has to feed two children aged 18 months. The food goes everywhere, including down her top! During the afternoon, Lisa has to clean up spilt water and paint from the painting activity. 'Well at least I'm not wearing my best jeans,' she thinks to herself as she looks in the mirror.

▷ Wearing a uniform has some clear benefits – what do you think they are?

The sight of a uniform can be reassuring. Service users get to know the uniform and, for example, may feel safe leaving their children in your care or during home care. Other benefits of wearing a uniform include:

- keeps your own clothes clean
- helps to provide a hygienic environment
- makes people feel 'they are in good hands'
- stops dress competition in low-paid jobs.

Skills development

The benefit of working in any kind of employment is developing new skills and new knowledge. When we are successful in gaining a new job, we are given the opportunity to learn the skills attached to that job. If we take work in early years, for example, we will learn about child development, child care, family care, play, and ourselves!

The way we learn all this new information is through a range of different techniques that include:

- learning on the job (i.e. copying other people)
- attending formal learning opportunities (perhaps a college)
- learning through books, magazines and journals
- learning through audio visual techniques (e.g. videos).

Whatever you need to learn, your teachers, supervisors and line managers can help you to gain the necessary knowledge and skills. Remember that the people you work with, often in teams, are also an important source of learning.

Once you have gained new skills and knowledge, you become a very 'marketable commodity'. In other words, other employers will want you to work for them!

CASE STUDY qualification and promotion

Ahmed has just completed his NVQ Level 2 in Care. He has been caring for older people in their own homes for about 14 months now. He has been promoted to team leader in his organisation, which means an increased salary and he now helps to train other people.

It is clear that Ahmed has gained benefits from training and qualifying in his chosen profession. Discuss with another person what these benefits might mean to Ahmed.

An increase in pay will help Ahmed to look after his family and run his home more successfully. However, having the qualification will also help Ahmed 'pick and choose' between employers. He can also look around to see who pays the most and who provides the best workplace.

Induction and training

The following information relates to starting work and what happens in the first few days, weeks and months of your new job.

Organisational structure

When you first start in a new job, you need to find out as much about the organisation as you can so that you can see where your job role fits into place.

All organisational structures are different. Some are hierarchical, which means there are layers of staff in different positions. The staff in these positions have different responsibilities. For example, the more senior staff tend to line manage the more junior staff. Nancy's Day Care Centre for children is a useful example of a hierarchy in the workplace (see below).

Board members and Chief Executive

Senior Manager

Team leader (2 to 4 years)   **Team leader (0 to 2 years)**

Nursery nurse **Nursery nurse** **Nursery nurse** **Nursery nurse**

The above example shows a hierarchical management structure. Each member of staff is responsible to a line manager who delegates the daily work routines. This is just one example of an organisational structure; there are many more, for example, the structure of a busy hospital ward (see overleaf). All of these structures can be written down or turned into charts, so that the staff can understand the management system used in their workplace.

It is important to remember that organisational structures often include full-time and part-time staff. This means that the staff are not available at all the times the organisation is working. For example, three members of the staff nurse team on the ward are employed part-time. Between them they only cover 50 hours a week. The ward sister has to make sure that she organises their working hours to ensure the smooth running of the ward.

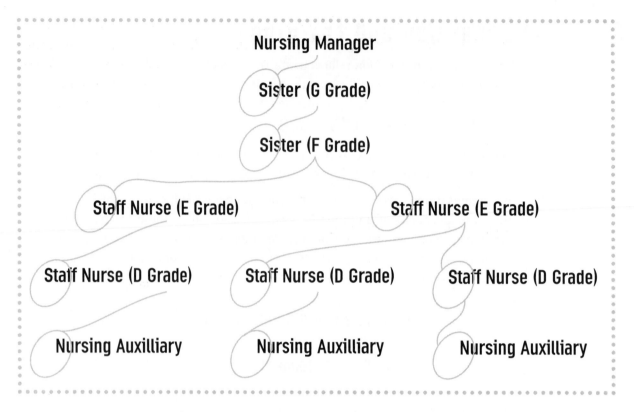

• • • *The department*

In the example of the hospital ward, we can see that the ward is the equivalent of a department. A department or division is a section of an organisation that specialises in some aspect of care. The ward we have looked at is a 'General Medical Ward'. If you work in a department, you will probably find that your skills and knowledge relate directly to the department you are employed in. It is usually only the big care organisations that have departments, such as hospitals, nursing homes and very large residential units.

GIVE IT A GO   working in a department

Find out about the different departments in your local hospital trust or health centre. Leaflets are usually a good source of information. Make a display that explains the role of two of the departments.

• • • *The team*

Teams are a very common way of working in the health, social care and early years sectors. A team is a group of people who work together to make sure that a task or job is completed successfully. Teams usually have a team leader with other members of staff taking on other roles, for example, marketing a service, looking after toy libraries, staff training and equal opportunities policies.

In many areas there are Sure Start centres. Sure Start is a government initiative that aims to help children get the best possible start in life. Most Sure Start centres have staff who are organised into teams. These could be classed as the early years team, the childminders network team, and so on. Many health professionals are also arranged in teams, for example, health visiting team, midwifery team and district nursing team.

GIVE IT A GO | Sure Start centres

Find out where your nearest Sure Start centre is. Use the Internet to help you and download information relating to the different teams.

People working in teams need to develop positive working relationships. A good working relationship involves:

- being professional and getting the job done
- being as helpful as possible to all team members
- valuing the work of every team member
- having your own work valued
- being respectful to all team members
- being well-organised and prepared for your work
- always being on time and working the hours required.

A visit

You may be asked (or invited) to visit the employing organisation before starting your job. A member of staff will usually show you around the premises and introduce you to the staff and clients using the service.

The benefits of visiting your new workplace before starting work are likely to be huge. For example:

- knowing what to expect
- meeting some of the clients
- meeting some of the staff
- having a general idea of the layout of the premises
- having a 'feel' for the organisation.

GIVE IT A GO | visit a workplace

Try and arrange to visit a workplace in your area to see what you can learn from the experience.

CASE STUDY | visiting before starting

Soreena was feeling rather nervous as she rang the doorbell of Anytown Care Home. Sister Jepson opened the door and welcomed her in. 'Come on,' she said, 'I will show you around. This is the main day lounge where our clients come to sit and watch the television.' Sister Jepson then introduced Joan who was watching a morning programme on the television. Next they went to the quiet room. 'This is where our clients come when they want to read or just feel like peace and quiet,' said Sister Jepson. As they went through the hallway, Sister Jepson pointed to two doors and said, 'These are the flats of Brian and Basil, they come out and join us when they want to.' The tour continued with a visit to the kitchen, the staff room, more small, self-contained flats and several bedrooms, as well as the games room and bar. Soreena felt quite confused with trying to learn the names of everyone she had met and all the places she had visited.

▷ Discuss with another student what the benefits might be to Soreena and the organisation of her making a visit before starting work.

● ● ● *A talk*

Another way to find out about a new workplace is to attend a talk. This may be given by a senior member of staff in the organisation to explain how the company works and the line management system. It is usually carried out for new staff within a few days of starting work and is part of what is often called an 'induction' programme.

Who to report to

This is very important information when starting work. Very often when you receive a letter telling you that you have been successful in gaining a job, the letter will tell you who to report to on arrival.

CASE STUDY | the first day

Taka has just started a new job as an administrator. She is feeling very nervous as she does not know anyone. Her letter said she has to report to Ms Pratt on arrival at work. She knocks on the main door and waits to be let in. The carer answering the door asks her what she wants. When she asks to be taken to Ms Pratt, the carer said, 'Oh, are you Taka who is starting work with us today? We are so glad you are here.'

▷ Working with another student, discuss how the carer will have made Taka feel. What are the benefits of having someone to report to when you first start work?

Once you have started work you might be given a line manager or supervisor. This could be someone different from the person you reported to on your first day. The person you report to often has several responsibilities in relation to your work, for example:

A supervisor talks to a new employee.

- telling you what tasks and duties you have to do
- advising on dress or uniform
- providing advice on expected behaviour
- recommending training programmes for you
- helping you to settle in to the workplace
- making sure you complete your induction programme
- working out the hours you need to work
- helping you to settle into the team
- introducing you to clients and their needs.

Expected behaviour

When working in health, social care and early years you will be expected to:

- behave professionally at all times
- keep clients and organisational information confidential
- demonstrate the care value base in all aspects of your work
- know when to ask for help
- keep yourself and your work environment clean and hygienic.

● ● ● *The care value base*

All who work in health, social care and early years need to develop a set of principles of good practice to help provide the kind of care each individual client or patient requires. These principles are called the *care value base*. They describe the kind of attitude towards care that you would appreciate if you were being cared for as a patient or client.

The main basis for the care value base is showing respect for each person as an individual. Care workers also have a responsibility to show respect towards other members of the care team with whom they are working.

••• *Respect in practice*

The main basis of the care value base: showing respect.

When you work in care, you are working with people who may be ill, have problems in their personal lives or simply need your help and support. It is particularly important for these people to be respected, even if they may sometimes make life difficult for their carers! Respect takes many different forms; look at the example in the picture opposite.

Respect for a client is the essential part of caring. If a carer cannot demonstrate this, then they may be in the wrong job! A carer should be able to put aside their own attitudes when caring for others if that attitude gets in the way of caring with respect.

••• *The principle of the care value base*

In the early 1990s, a group of professional care workers met to decide what kind of care values all care workers should bring to their work. Carers who work with these values in mind not only give clients the respect they deserve, but also help clients to have confidence and trust in all care workers.

The care value base has three main parts:

1 **Making sure that the services promote and foster people's rights and responsibilities**. The service provider (e.g. health or social services) has a responsibility to make sure that clients know about the services available to them and can access these services. Each carer also has a responsibility to make sure that the client is able to continue having the care he or she needs for as long as is necessary.

2 **Supporting and promoting equality and diversity**. All clients should be given the care they need according to their individual health and care requirements. That is, everyone should have an equal opportunity to receive care and support, regardless of their colour, age, sex (male or female), culture, religion, sexual orientation, illness or disability.

3 **Maintaining the confidentiality of information**. Keeping information confidential – i.e. not telling others what people tell you about themselves – is a very important part of care. It enables your client to trust you and have confidence in you as their carer. Your relationship with your client depends on trust.

Sometimes you may have to tell a more senior worker or manager about information you receive, for example, when you believe that a client or other people are at risk. This is the only time when you should pass on confidential information.

GIVE IT A GO the care value base

With another student, read the following three cases, each one describing a situation that relates to the care value base. Match each case to the value base represented.

☐ Nan and her friend Jack are waiting to see the physiotherapist at the local health centre when two staff come in having a loud conversation about one of their clients. Nan knows the client – she was the friend of her neighbour. The staff talk about personal matters relating to the client's family. Although Nan 'coughs' to let them know they are there, the staff members keep on talking. Nan has to walk away because she is so embarrassed.

☐ Samina has been taken into respite care for two weeks. She has asked her carer for a private place to pray, to be used at least three times during the day. She is happy to use her bedroom in the morning and again at night, but she cannot get back to her room without help. The carer finds Samina a quiet room and always comes to collect her in time to help her get to the prayer room.

☐ Ted is about to be discharged from hospital after a hip replacement. He is quite worried because he doesn't know how he will cope, and nobody has had the time to talk to him. His wife is quite active, but he doesn't want her rushing around after him. The nurse who is packing up Ted's belongings notices that he seems worried. When she asks him what the problem is, he explains his concerns. The nurse realises that for some reason Ted was not given the discharge advice which is usual after an operation. She then spends time with Ted explaining everything to him and uses a booklet with illustrations. Ted is much less worried and now feels confident that he will cope at home.

Clothes and uniform

When working in the care sector, you will most likely be asked to wear a uniform. In most cases, the uniform will be provided for you (you will not need to pay for it). You will probably be given as many as three sets of uniform so that you can have one being laundered, one to wear and one ready for wearing in case of emergency changes.

Some job roles also require special shoes. Where this is the case, you may be offered finance towards the cost of your shoes. However, it is usual for most footwear to be flat and comfortable because you are likely to be on your feet most of the time. If you have a job that requires you to move or handle clients and equipment, flat shoes are even more important for safety reasons.

Health and safety training

• • • Fire

Fire is a major danger in all health, social care and early years settings. Can you imagine how difficult it would be to safely evacuate all the clients from a busy hospital if a large fire was to break out at night? Nurses and other staff require special training to help them evacuate bed-bound patients safely and efficiently.

Most healthcare settings now operate a 'no smoking policy'. This is intended to:

- improve the health of clients
- reduce the amount of passive smoking (breathing in other people's tobacco smoke)
- cut down the cost of redecorating (nicotine stains on walls and furniture)
- most especially, to cut down the risk of fire.

We have to trust people to obey the rules of a workplace. Unfortunately, those rules are often broken and hazardous situations then develop. Keeping your clients, colleagues, workplace and yourself safe from fire is not an easy task. You will need to think about all the situations that could lead to fire breaking out, including:

- naked lights
- cooking methods
- electrical wiring
- clients who smoke.

- natural heating fires
- electrical equipment
- gas or oxygen cylinders

GIVE IT A GO fire risks

Working with another student, identify those causes of fire that could apply in your own place of work or the centre where you are studying. Make notes of your discussions.

Knowing what to do in the event of a fire is the very first stage of keeping everyone safe from harm. If you or your colleagues do not know what to do in your workplace, then everyone is at risk from serious injury or even death.

• • • *Moving and handling people and equipment*

Moving people and equipment is definitely a hazard in the workplace. It is important for carers to make sure that they have had appropriate training before they try to move or handle people or equipment. It is far too easy to damage your back because you do not know how to move and handle people and equipment safely. Factors which can make carers more likely to injure their backs are:

- lifting patients
- working in an awkward, unstable or crouched position, including bending forward, sideways or twisting the body
- lifting loads at arm's length
- lifting with a standing and finishing position near the floor, overhead or at arm's length
- lifting an uneven load with the weight on the side
- handling an uncooperative or falling patient.

There are many risks associated with lifting and handling things, such as:

- injury to the carer
- injury to the client
- dropping expensive equipment and breaking it
- injury to people around us
- loss of job and income
- loss of confidence.

Moving and handling should never be carried out until you have had the proper, recognised training. Carers often find themselves being asked to assist a client with a movement. In these cases, it is important that you are trained to move the person safely. If you have never had any training, ask your employer or supervisor to show you how it can be done safely.

When working with babies and small children it might be difficult to eliminate all manual handling. However, it is still important to avoid or reduce the risk of injury. Take the same precautions to move and handle children and babies as you would with any other client.

• • • *Dangerous substances*

Substances come in many different forms, some of which are chemicals. It is very likely that some of the substances that you regularly use in the home or workplace are capable of burning the skin or causing breathing difficulties if inhaled (breathing in the fumes). Many substances are only harmful if used wrongly. If you follow the manufacturer's instructions you will keep yourself, your colleagues and your clients safe from accidental harm. The kinds of substances you are most likely to come across in a care setting are shown in the diagram overleaf.

Sickness procedures

Another essential piece of information that you will need when you start work is what to do if you are sick and need time off work. When you have responsibility for the care of other people, it is especially important to let your line manager or supervisor know as soon as possible that you cannot come to work. You should:

- telephone your place of employment to let them know immediately
- if you are off work for more than three days, complete a self-certification form which must be given to your workplace
- if you are off work for more than seven days, get a sickness certificate from your doctor which must be sent to your workplace
- when you are ready to return to work your doctor will need to give you a 'fit for work certificate', which must be given to your employer on return.

It is very helpful to an employer to keep him or her informed of your progress whilst you are off work, so that plans can be made to cover your work.

Arranging annual leave

Most employers will expect you to arrange your time off in advance so they can arrange for your colleagues or external staff to cover your job role while you are away. When you work in a team, the whole team usually needs to agree who is going on holiday and when, so that two people are not away at the same time.

Formal induction

All of the issues we have considered in this section are part of the formal induction that you will be given when you start work in health, social care and early years. However, if you are going to work in social care there is a requirement to complete the Care Induction Training within six weeks of starting work. There are five standards that have to be completed. These are:

1 Understand the principles of care.

2 Understand the organisation and the worker role.

3 Understand the experiences and the particular needs of the service user groups.

4 Maintain safety at work.

5 Understand the effects of the service setting on service provision.

This leads to a qualification in its own right and your compliance will be inspected as part of the inspection process for the care setting.

◼◼◼ EVIDENCE ACTIVITY

Preparing an induction pack

Candace is starting work at the same care home as you. She has been told that she will be given an induction pack on her first day. As her more experienced work colleague you have been asked to prepare the induction pack for her. Your manager has asked you to make sure it includes:

▷ a description of the purposes of induction

▷ an explanation of why induction is important to both Candace and your care home

▷ an explanation of how induction will take place in your place of work

▷ an explanation for Candace of how the induction process will help her to understand her terms and conditions of work.

◼ ◼ ◼ ◼ Procedures used to monitor performance

An important part of working in health, social care and early years is the procedures used to monitor your performance. In other words, the steps taken to check how well you are carrying out your job. In many workplaces, rewards are given to people who work well and achieve in all aspects of their job. Rewards vary from organisation to organisation but could include bonus payments, staff development opportunities or extension of a temporary contract.

The procedures used to monitor performance also vary, but generally include:

- appraisal
- quality standards
- assessment.

Appraisal

Appraisal is a system for measuring an employee's performance. An individual's line manager or supervisor usually carries out an appraisal once a year (although in some organisations it can be more frequent). In an ideal situation, both the appraiser (the person carrying out the appraisal) and the appraisee (the person being appraised) will have had training beforehand to explain how the appraisal system works and when it should be carried out.

The appraisal system can be informal or formal. Whichever method is used, the main purposes of appraisal are:

- to identify an employee's strengths
- to identify an employees' needs for development
- to decide if an increase in salary should be paid
- to see who might be ready for promotion
- to find out what training might be required
- to aid the communication process within the organisation
- to help the organisation plan their staffing needs.

When you have an appraisal you are given the chance to talk about your work and progress on a one-to-one basis with your line manager or supervisor. This is your chance to demonstrate how good you are at your job. It is also your supervisor's opportunity to give you feedback on how well you are doing your job. If you or your supervisor feel that more training is required, your appraisal is the time to discuss this and agree options for the future.

CASE STUDY — An appraisal

Simon is having his first appraisal with Polly his supervisor. He has filled in the questionnaire she gave him about how he feels he is doing at work. She has filled one in about how she sees his work. Simon is nervous about the meeting because he wants to tell Polly that he would like more responsibility now that he has been working there for one year, but he is not sure if she will agree.

▷ Discuss with another student the benefits of filling in a questionnaire that asks you to think about your work in preparation for the appraisal.

CASE STUDY) An appraisal continued

When Simon and Polly meet, she asks him to sit down and explains the process they will be following. She tells him he has an hour to discuss all the relevant issues with her. She asks him to begin by telling her how he feels about his job. Simon is enthusiastic and it quickly becomes clear to Polly that Simon loves his job and would like to do more to help the organisation to achieve its objectives of caring for people with physical disabilities.

◻   Make notes of the appraisal process so far. Don't forget to include the questionnaire stage.

Polly listens to Simon and when he has finished she tells him what she thinks about his work. She says how pleased she is with his performance, enthusiasm and willingness to help. His sickness record is excellent and he has proved himself to be reliable and hard working. She suggests that he might like to consider promotion and start an NVQ Level 3 at the local college in order to prepare for a change in his duties. Simon is delighted – he didn't even have to ask!

Simon's appraisal has gone very well; he has achieved everything he wanted. He came out of the office feeling as though he had been given a 'pat on the back'. However, his colleague Jane did not find the experience as pleasant. She started work at the same time as Simon but was always taking time off. She was known to be short tempered with both clients and colleagues. She has been given a warning to perform better in future and will need to be re-appraised in six weeks' time to see if there is a difference in her performance.

• • • *Confirm the role of the organisation*

Appraisal is another way of making sure that each individual employee knows and understands the purpose and mission of the organisation. During one-to-one discussions the supervisor can go over the main functions and tasks of the organisation and how the employee contributes to the achievement of these.

• • • *Re-employment and reputation*

In the care sector it is essential that an organisation has a good reputation. In many cases, clients trust you with their most treasured possessions, for example, children or even their lives. It is the staff working in an organisation that gives it its reputation, whether good or bad. Staff who do not meet the needs of the organisation will usually find that their employment is terminated (they lose their jobs).

Quality standards

These are very often external standards set by government bodies that allow an organisation to show how good it is in relation to some aspect of its performance. It also allows the government to benchmark an organisation and its performance against other, similar organisations.

• • • *TOPPS Induction and Foundation Standards*

These are the standards of competency that a new employee must reach within six months of starting a new job. The Standards relate to five areas of competence. The Induction Standards were considered earlier in the unit (see page 69). For the Foundation Stage you need to:

- understand how to apply the care value base
- communicate effectively
- develop as a worker
- recognise and respond to abuse and neglect
- understand the experiences and particular needs of the individuals using the service.

• • • *Qualifications*

In some professions you cannot get a job without being qualified. Some of these include:

- nursing
- social work
- early years education
- physiotherapy
- community psychiatric nursing.

• • • *National Occupational Standards*

These standards are perhaps best known as National Vocational Qualifications (NVQs, or SVQs in Scotland). These have been in place since the middle of the 1980s but it is only now that there is a legal requirement for social care organisations to make sure that their staff are trained and qualified to the appropriate level.

National Occupational Standards relate directly to the job that a person does. For example, the NVQ in Care contains a number of units, each one stating the competency (performance criteria) required to do that part of the work.

• • • *ISO9000*

Whilst you may come across this Quality Standard in some care settings, in general it relates more closely to production and administration activities. However, now is a good opportunity to find out more about it.

GIVE IT A GO ISO9000

Use the Internet to find out more about ISO9000. Make notes of your findings.

• • • Investors in People

Investors in People is a very popular quality standard that allows an organisation to demonstrate to the outside world how much it values and 'invests' in its staff. The organisation has to demonstrate to external inspectors the ways in which it encourages staff development. This normally includes evidence of robust appraisal systems and staff development.

Assessment

The quality standards we have looked at up to now are a form of assessment but we can take this a little further by exploring specific forms of assessment.

• • • Self-assessment

Self-assessment is exactly as it sounds: it is when an individual makes a judgement about his or her ability in the workplace. Do you remember Simon filling in the questionnaire about his work before he had his appraisal (page 70)? That is classed as self-assessment.

Some people keep logs of their progress in the workplace. This is like a diary and allows new employees to make notes about things they may need help with or the things they are feeling confident about. This log can be used to discuss performance with a supervisor.

• • • Assessment by a line manager

We saw Simon being assessed by his line manager, Polly. This we called an appraisal. Appraisal is a formal method of assessment but assessment by a line manager can also be informal.

CASE STUDY) informal assessment

Nusrat has been working in the under-fours day nursery for three weeks. She thoroughly enjoys the work. Today she is cleaning the room ready for storytime. She makes sure that the toys that can cause a distraction are removed and that the carpet is clean and safe for the children to sit on. 'Thank you,' says her line manager, 'that's a job well done!'

Discuss with another student the difference between this feedback and the feedback Simon received (on page 71).

This feedback is instant; Nusrat's line manager is demonstrating encouragement as well as 'on the job, informal assessment'. In Simon's case, the assessment was more formal: both him and his supervisor had had time to think about what was going to be said and what the results might be. In Simon's appraisal the feedback was probably written down and stored in his staff records. In Nusrat's case, however, the feedback would be 'lost' because it was not written down.

GIVE IT A GO — written feedback

Working with another person, discuss the advantages and disadvantages of having feedback written down.

• • • *Peer assessment*

This kind of assessment, whilst useful, is full of dangers and pitfalls. Peer assessment is where a colleague at the same level as yourself in the organisation gives you feedback on your work, or you give a colleague feedback on his or her performance. Peer assessment can be used as part of a wider assessment (such as appraisal). If peer assessment is to be used, the employer will need to think about:

- staff training
- level of ability
- level of understanding
- working relationships.

Peer assessment can be used informally, perhaps during a meeting, but this is not always the best place to air your views. When feedback is good it is fine to praise people publicly. However, if your assessment is poor it may be better to give your opinion in private.

CASE STUDY — giving opinions in private

Peter is taking part in a team meeting to review how the last inspection went. During the meeting the agenda moves on to discuss staff roles during the inspection. Peter's colleague Anna says that she felt that Peter taking time off during the inspection was not helpful; he had left her trying to cover two jobs whilst an inspector was checking client care. No wonder they were given a poor report!

▷ Working with another person, discuss how you think this might have made Peter feel. How else could the issue have been handled?

The importance of monitoring performance

The importance of monitoring performance in a care establishment should not be under-estimated. If an organisation allows poor performance to continue 'unchecked', it is likely to find that its business will be closed, either because external inspectors will say it is not fit to look after clients or because clients will not use the service.

• • • *Protection for all*

Monitoring performance is a way of making sure that clients receive the best possible service. Clients are best protected when qualified, competent staff are involved in their everyday care. Well-qualified and competent staff are a joy to work with: their colleagues can trust their actions and know that their own safety is protected.

• • • *Improved performance*

The main aim of any care service is to provide the highest quality care to its service users. This can only be achieved if the organisation and the individuals working in it are committed to year-on-year improvement. Any individual or organisation that fails to continually improve will eventually be left behind!

• • • *Regulations*

One of the other reasons for monitoring individual and organisational performance is because it is a requirement by law. In the past, care homes and other services have been condemned for providing poor quality service to their users, sometimes leading to the deaths of clients. When this happens, the government 'steps in' to establish legal regulations to ensure high-quality service at all times.

• • • *Other procedures*

There are other procedures in the workplace that are designed to create a safe working environment, and to ensure that your rights are protected and that clients and other staff are protected from another person's incompetence. These procedures include:

- grievance procedures
- disciplinary procedures
- health and safety.

We have already discussed health and safety on pages 66–68.

• • • *Grievance*

A grievance can be 'taken out' by any employee who feels that they have been treated unfairly. This unfair treatment can relate to a whole range of different things, for example:

- a breach of confidentiality
- unfair criticism
- bullying
- poor line management
- the wrong rate of pay.

These are just a few examples, and each grievance has to be taken on its merits.

If the organisation has a personnel department, they would normally help the person with the grievance to take action. This usually means:

1 Writing the complaint (grievance) down.

2 Giving it to a senior person to make a judgement about what should happen.

3 If you agree with the judgement, then action is taken.

4 If you do not agree with the judgement, the grievance is passed to a more senior person for him or her to make a judgement.

5 If you agree with the judgement, action is taken.

6 If you still do not agree with the judgement, then the grievance may need to be taken to an external person for agreement to be reached.

In most cases, an organisation will try to solve the problem as quickly and in the earliest stages as possible. It is unpleasant trying to work with a grievance that either you or another person has raised. However, sometimes a grievance is unavoidable, especially if client care is likely to be affected.

••• *Disciplinary procedures*

Disciplinary procedures are sometimes the result of a grievance! A disciplinary is a written record of an individual continuing to provide poor or inappropriate work performance. Generally, a disciplinary stays on an employee's record for 12 months (or longer in some cases). If further disciplinary action is taken during the year, the employee can be dismissed.

Sometimes, an employee is guilty of gross misconduct (behaviour considered extremely inappropriate). Examples of gross misconduct could include:

- endangering a client's life
- failing to protect a client
- fraud.
- abuse
- theft

When these occur, an employee can be dismissed immediately.

⬤⬤⬤ EVIDENCE ACTIVITY

Monitoring performance

The Happy Days Nursery is holding their monthly staff meeting. On the agenda is 'monitoring work'. You have been asked to attend this meeting to give a presentation about why it is important to monitor work in early years care. The presentation can be either written, verbal or visual.

In the presentation, you should describe at least one example of a procedure used for monitoring work, giving examples of how work procedures are used to monitor individual performance. Finally, you should explain to the group the importance of monitoring performance to the employer, the employee and the service user (customer).

unit 3

Developing skills in health and social care

In this unit you will learn about the practical skills necessary for work in the health, social care and early years sectors. You will find out about people's physical, social and emotional needs at different times in their lives. You will learn about different types of communication and how to show that you respect and value all people through the way that you communicate.

You will discover the importance of independence for individuals and learn how to encourage independence skills for people of all ages. You will investigate what is meant by personal care and explore the skills required to assist people in a dignified and respectful manner.

In this unit you will learn about:

▷ people's needs at different times throughout their lives
▷ developing good relationships by using communication to respect and value individuals
▷ possible ways to encourage independence for different groups
▷ what is meant by personal care and how this can be supported.

People's needs throughout their lives

Physical, social and emotional needs

People have basic human needs which must be met in order to survive. These are often described as physical needs, social needs and emotional needs.

- **Physical needs:**
  These are the things that a person needs to keep the body alive, including fresh air, food and drink, sleep, rest and exercise. Shelter is also required because people need to be kept safe from harm and protected from danger.
- **Social or belonging needs:**
  Everyone needs to feel that they belong; that they are welcome and accepted by other people. They need to feel loved and needed by family and friends.
- **Emotional or self-esteem needs:**
  People need to feel good about themselves, and feel that they are respected and valued by other people.

Maslow's hierarchy of human needs

During the 1960s, a psychologist called Abraham Maslow who was working in America decided that some human needs were more important than others were. He described what he called a 'hierarchy of human needs'. This means that some basic needs must be met before others are. The diagram opposite shows Maslow's hierarchy, with the most important needs at the bottom of the pyramid and those least essential to human survival at the top.

• • • *Physical needs*

Without air a body will die very quickly. It is no use being loved if you cannot breathe, so the need for air must be more important than love. A body can live for many weeks without food, but cannot survive without water for more than a few days. So water becomes more important than food for human survival.

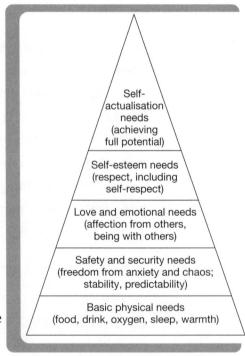

Maslow's hierarchy of human needs.

• • • *The need for safety and security*

We know that without air, food and water a person will quickly die. However, once these needs are met, people then realise that they need to feel safe and secure. For example, we make the environment safe by wearing seat belts in the car, putting locks on the doors and taking care not to be out alone at night.

• • • *The need for love and emotional support*

Once a person has all their basic physical and security needs met, he or she is able to find another layer: the need for belonging. People need to be loved and find friends, to have affectionate relationships and become part of a community.

• • • *The need to develop self-esteem*

Once people have achieved a good feeling of belonging, they discover that they need to have good self-esteem – to feel good about themselves, e.g. how they look and the kind of person they are.

• • • *Self-actualisation and reaching potential by achieving goals*

Finally, once a person has developed good self-esteem, he or she may be able to feel that he or she is achieving full potential – this is known as 'self-actualisation'.

▣▣▣ EVIDENCE ACTIVITY

Basic human needs

Describe how your physical, social and emotional needs have been met this week. Consider, food and drink, rest, sleep and exercise, safety, belonging and friendship, self-esteem and achievement.

Maslow identified that people do not remain at the same level in the hierarchy throughout life. If people are in a stressful situation, they may move down to a lower level. For example, if you fail an exam, lose your job or a relationship breaks down, your self-esteem is lower and what you need most is the love and support of friends and family – the feeling of belonging. If a young person runs away from home, is alone and feels that no one cares, what becomes important is keeping safe and finding enough food and drink to survive.

It is easy to see that people become ill if they do not have enough food and water or are not kept safe. It is perhaps not so easy to understand that people who do not feel good about themselves or do not have a good feeling of belonging can also become ill, both mentally and physically.

CASE STUDY meeting basic needs

Agnes is 82 years old. She used to be a teacher and when she retired she became involved in the local church where she ran the Sunday school and the luncheon club. She was proud of her ability to help others and still be so active at 82 years of age. Her sons both lived locally and she enjoyed seeing them and her grandchildren regularly. Last year her eldest son and his family moved to America and her second son died. Then, after breaking her leg, Agnes could no longer manage at home and had to go into a nursing home. She is not happy now as she can't do all the things she used to do and no longer sees her friends and family. Her favourite time of the day is mealtimes. Each morning the first thing she asks is, 'What's for dinner today?'

▷ When do you think that Agnes achieved her full potential?

▷ Do you think that Agnes used to have good self-esteem? Why?

▷ How do you know that Agnes used to have a feeling of belonging?

▷ Why does Agnes get so much pleasure from her food?

Different needs at different times

People's basic needs differ at different times of their lives.

Age/stage	Physical needs	Social needs	Emotional needs
Babies 0–2 years	Fresh air (no smoke). Regular food and drink. To be kept warm. Good hygiene. To be safe and secure. Sleep, rest and exercise.	People to pay them attention. People to act as role models.	To be loved and cared for by a few main carers.
Children 2–10 years	As above.	To play and make friends. To encourage a feeling of belonging.	To feel valued and respected. To develop good self-esteem. Opportunities to learn and achieve. Independence.
Adolescents 10–18 years	As above.	Wide circle of friends. To explore relationships and sexual behaviour.	Extra support to develop self-esteem which may be difficult during adolescence. To be more independent of parents and family.
Adults 18–65 years	As above.	A supportive relationship. Friends to share interests with.	The opportunity to work and earn a living. To achieve self-actualisation.
Senior citizens 65+ years	As above. If health fails, may need help with dressing, eating, walking and keeping safe.	As above. May lose friends and partners and be lonely.	All of the above plus the ability to remain independent.

The physical, social and emotional needs of babies, children, adolescents, adults and senior citizens.

⬛⬛⬤ EVIDENCE ACTIVITY

Needs at different stages of life

Isobel is 1 year old. She lives with her 6-year-old brother Jason and her mother Laura. Laura looks after her 81-year-old grandmother who lives next door.

▷ Make a poster to put in your file describing the needs of each person.

You have seen that a person's needs differ throughout their life. In addition, every individual may also have different needs.

CASE STUDY · meeting individual needs

Imagine a class of 8-year-old children eating a school dinner. You might think that they all have the same need for food. However:

▷ Jasmine has diabetes and has to limit the amount of sugar that she eats.

▷ Jamilla is a Muslim and only eats halal food.

▷ Justine is allergic to peanuts so all food must be checked to ensure that there are no traces of nuts.

▷ Joseph hates custard.

▷ Jack has a very big appetite and likes to eat a lot.

▷ Jarina has a small appetite and never finishes her food.

▷ Joel has cerebral palsy and cannot use a knife and fork to eat his food.

All of these 8-year-old children have very different needs.

1 Do you think that you can treat all these children the same?

2 What might happen if you did this?

3 What are you going to do for each child to meet their individual needs?

• • • *What does this mean for the work of the carer?*

As a professional carer, you cannot treat everyone the same: you need to meet each individual person's needs. Carers meet individual needs in the following ways:

Find out what the person needs

Provide a service to meet these needs

Meeting individual needs

Value and respect all people

Refer people for help when you cannot meet their needs

• • • *The rights of all individuals to have their needs met*

Government legislation requires that individuals have the right to have their needs met. Some of the laws that address the needs and rights of children and adults are:

- the Children Act 1989
- the Care Standards Act 2000
- the Human Rights Act 1998
- the Race Relations Act 1976
- the Disability Discrimination Act 2000.

The government makes the law and organisations decide how they will implement the law. They do this by creating policies and procedures which describe how employees must work to meet the client's individual needs.

The United Nations Convention on the Rights of the Child identifies that children have a right to:

- enough food and clean water
- an adequate standard of living
- be kept safe
- healthcare
- be protected from abuse.

CASE STUDY) meeting the needs of all individuals

▢ Jasmine is 3 years old. Her mum lets her play out on the pavement by a busy road.

▢ Mr Green lives in a Nursing Home. He has developed a bladder infection and needs to go to the toilet very often. On Saturday the staff were busy organising the Christmas party so nobody came when Mr Green needed the toilet.

▢ Joe has learning difficulties and lives in a supported housing unit. His carers have found that it is much quicker to dress him in the morning rather than wait while he tries to do it himself.

1 What are the specific needs of each of these people?

2 Describe what will happen if their individual needs are not met.

3 State why it is important that they should have their needs met.

Communication to show respect and value for all people

What is communication?

Communication is about how we interact with other people. It is a two-way process which includes giving information to and receiving information from other people. This information can be exchanged or passed on either verbally or non-verbally.

● ● ● *Verbal communication*

Verbal communication describes sharing information using the spoken word.

● ● ● *Non-verbal communication*

Non-verbal communication is communicating without the use of the spoken word, i.e. using gestures, body movements and facial expressions.

Different groups of people may communicate in different ways. For example, babies do not use words but communicate with sounds, facial expressions and body language. People with a hearing disability may use sign language to communicate. This means using a series of hand and body gestures which make up a complete language system.

GIVE IT A GO — non-verbal communication

The next time you are with a group of people, quietly observe them for a short time. You will see that they:

▷ use their hands to gesture

▷ use the face to show expressions

▷ use the body to lean forward, lie back or turn away.

1 Make a list of all the different non-verbal signals you can see during communication.

2 Share the following information with a friend without using words:

▷ Come here.   ▷ I'm hungry.   ▷ I'm bored.

For further information about communication, see pages 194–196.

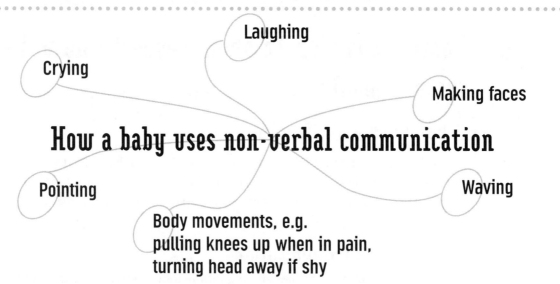

In different languages there may be a different emphasis on gestures and non-verbal communication. You probably communicate in different ways with different groups of people.

WHAT  — Communicating with different groups

...You were asked if you communicate in different ways?

Describe any differences in your communication with these different groups: a baby, your parents, your friends, your teachers.

Getting the message across

To find out what people need and then meet their needs, you must develop very good communication skills. The way that people speak has a direct effect on the way that the message is heard and responded to. Some of the factors that affect the meaning of spoken words are:

- the volume
- the speed
- the tone of voice.

GIVE IT A GO tone of voice

1 Working with a friend, practise saying 'Do you want a cup of tea?' in the following ways:

   ▷ speaking loudly as though you were angry

   ▷ speaking very fast as though you were in a hurry

   ▷ speaking calmly and gently.

   Ask your friend to reply to each different question.

   How did the way you asked the question affect the answer your friend gave?

2 Mr Jones is deaf. People shout at him all the time. How do you think that makes him feel?

Communication always includes verbal and non-verbal messages. You use eye contact to attract the attention of the person you want to talk to and hold his or her attention. You use facial expression to show interest by nodding or smiling, and to show understanding and emotion.

GIVE IT A GO eye contact and facial expression

Working with a friend:

▷ Both look at the floor. Tell your friend all about what you did last weekend.

▷ Ask your friend to tell you about her weekend. This time you can look at each other while you talk.

1 Did the conversation last any longer when you were both looking at each other?

2 What did it feel like when you were talking to someone who was not looking at you?

3 What did you learn by looking at your friend while he or she was talking to you?

• • • How different emotions can be communicated

As a professional carer, it is important that you recognise how people communicate their emotions. People communicate emotions consciously (knowing that they are doing it) and unconsciously (unaware that they are doing it).

• • • Conscious and unconscious communication

It is fairly easy to recognise if someone is happy or sad if that person tells you directly how he or she is feeling. However, it may not be so easy to spot how someone is feeling if he or she does not tell you directly. Vulnerable people who need care often do not say how they are feeling. It may be that they do not want to be a bother or that they think you will not be interested in their problems. Children do not have the language to explain what they feel. You therefore need to be able to identify what people are feeling.

CASE STUDY) body language

Look at the picture below and find someone who is comforting a sad person, someone who is angry, someone who is bored and someone who wants attention.

How do you know what these people are feeling?

People communicate their feelings in the following ways

- consciously through:
  - language, using words like angry, worried, jealous
  - touch, hugs and cuddles, holding hands
- unconsciously through:
  - facial expressions like frowning, scowling, looking puzzled
  - body language such as fidgeting, clenched fists
  - behaviour such as being withdrawn or aggressive.

• • • *Body language*

From the drawing on page 86 and your observations of people, you can see that the way we use our body gives out messages about how we are feeling.

Respect and values

In order to develop a good relationship with your clients, you need to demonstrate that you respect and value them. Clients may need your help for aspects of personal care so it is particularly important to treat people with dignity and respect.

GIVE IT A GO   showing respect

Name three people who you respect and whose opinion you value. How do you show that you respect them?

Helping to build good relationships	Hindering the development of good relationships
Making time for people to talk	Ignoring people or rushing away
Finding out what people like to be called and using their correct name	Calling people names, mocking or teasing them
Listening carefully	Interrupting
Showing that you are interested by watching their faces, nodding and making encouraging noises such as 'Mmm', 'yes' or 'I see'	Thinking about or doing other things while talking to a client
Responding to what people are saying, perhaps asking a question to show that you have been listening	Ignoring people or just saying 'It will be alright don't worry about it'
Valuing and respecting other people's opinions even if you do not agree with them	Forcing your own opinion on others or laughing at other people's views
Acknowledging other people's feelings even if it is uncomfortable for you	Ignoring or walking away from a situation which may be embarrassing; the other person may need help
Using interpreters if people speak in a different language to you	Ignoring people who do not speak the same language as you do
Talking clearly or writing things down if people can't hear	Shouting at people who have a hearing difficulty

CASE STUDY — respectful communication

Read the following case studies. For each case study, answer the following questions:

1 What is wrong with the communication?

2 What is the effect on the adult or child?

3 What would you have said in that situation?

▷ When Mrs Jones brought Jemma in to nursery this morning, she said, 'I'm sorry we are late but my mother died last night', and she started to cry. The early years worker was embarrassed so quickly answered, 'Oh dear, I am sorry – well don't worry we will look after Jemma. Off you go, I am sure you must have lots to do.'

▷ Lorraine and Julie are putting Mrs Smith to bed. They are both busy talking about what they are going to do when they leave work tonight. Mrs Smith tries to tell them that she has a pain in her side. 'Oh don't worry,' snaps Julie, 'you always have something to complain about. It will be better in the morning.'

▷ It is dinner time at nursery. George has asked for some more food. 'No wonder you are such a fatty, Georgie Porgy,' Sharon says as she ladles out some more shepherd's pie.

▷ Jamilla and Shaheen are talking in Urdu as they play in the sand pit. Two members of staff pass by and one says, 'I wish they wouldn't talk in that stupid language. They will never learn English properly so long as they do.'

⬛⬛⬛ EVIDENCE ACTIVITY

Communication

Make a poster describing how communication can help or hinder the development of good relationships. List some barriers to communication.

Independence for difference groups

Personal independence is an essential part of life. People need to be independent in order to feel good about themselves, have good self-esteem and the ability to achieve. Your role is to encourage clients to be as independent as possible.

Why independence is important

You need to remember that there are different areas of independence: physical, emotional and economic.

- **Physical independence** includes the ability to feed oneself, carry out personal care routines (washing, dressing and toileting) and move around.
- **Emotional independence** includes being able to make decisions for yourself and establish positive social relationships.
- **Economic independence** includes the ability to earn money to support yourself or your family.

• • • *Emotional well-being*

Emotional well-being is about how we see ourselves and our ability to cope with life, make social relationships and develop emotional independence.

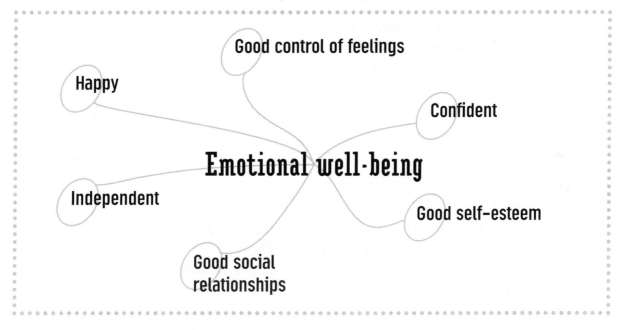

• • • *Self-esteem*

Self-esteem is about how you feel about yourself. Being independent is essential to the development of good self-esteem. A person who is not independent and has to rely on other people may find it difficult to feel good about him or herself.

CASE STUDY) improving a client's self-esteem

Freda has always allowed the care staff to dress her since it is much quicker for everyone. Last month a new carer called Yasmin arrived and she has been encouraging Freda to dress herself. She found Freda a long handled shoe-horn and a gadget for putting stockings on. Yesterday Yasmin was late and when she arrived Freda was sitting in her chair completely dressed and looking very pleased with herself.

▷ Why do you think that Freda was pleased with herself?

▷ How has this improved Freda's self-esteem and emotional well-being?

GIVE IT A GO | self-esteem

List things that you like about yourself and things that you do not like.

▷ Which list was easier to write?

▷ Do you think that you have good self-esteem?

● ● ● *Achievement*

There is also a strong link between independence and achievement. When a young boy first learns to do up his zip by himself, he feels that he has achieved and feels good about himself. This in turn encourages him to practise the next task and learn, for example, to tie up his own shoelaces, becoming more independent.

Everyone can achieve something each day, so it is important that you encourage the people you care for to achieve as much as they can within the limits of their abilities.

CASE STUDY | achievement

At Meadowsweet Care Home the staff provide recreational activities every day. They organise games, provide a range of craft activities and have a creative writing group where people write their life story. There is a computer class every Wednesday and a gardening club on Friday.

▷ List all of the ways that people can achieve while involved in recreational activities.

At Sunrise Supported Living Home, the clients who have learning difficulties go to classes at the local college every day.

▷ The clients enjoy going to college. Why do you think this is?

You can see from these examples that emotional well-being, self-esteem, independence and achievement are closely linked.

How independence can be encouraged

As a carer, you will encourage and support children and adults to enable them to become as independent as possible within the limits of their abilities. Encouraging independence means:

- setting tasks that are achievable
- agreeing how much support you will provide
- being patient
- giving people plenty of time
- providing praise and encouragement.

You may see clients using aids and gadgets provided by physiotherapists and occupational therapists, to support independence.

Mobility
Sticks, crutches, Zimmer frames, wheelchair

Eating
Wide-handled cutlery, plates with lips and mats to hold plates steady, two-handled mugs

Independence aids

Dressing
Long handled shoe-horns, gadgets to put on socks and tights, elastic shoelaces, gadgets to do up buttons, velcro fastenings

Cooking
Adapted kitchen utensils, gadgets to hold and tip kettles, a gadget to hang on a cup which sounds when the cup gets full

⬛⬛⬛ EVIDENCE ACTIVITY

Aids and gadgets for independent living

Using the Internet, find some aids and gadgets that encourage independent living. Possible sites are: www.benefitsnowshop.co.uk and http://freespace.virgin.net/whistling.tortoise/, but there are many others.

• • • *Negotiating the level of assistance required*

Before providing any help or care, you need to ask the client what he or she would like you to do and how much assistance is required.

Negotiating the level of assistance

...*You have been asked to help a client get dressed?*

You ask Jack what help he needs. He tells you that he cannot put on his shoes. You reply, 'I can put them on the floor beside your chair, making sure that they are undone. I can give you this long handled shoe-horn and you could try to put them on yourself. I'll tie up your laces for you. Tomorrow I will get you some elastic shoelaces so that, with a bit of practice, you can put your shoes on yourself.'

▷ Describe how the amount of help Jack needs to put on his shoes has been negotiated.

Sometimes clients may not want to do things for themselves. There are several reasons why an individual may not wish to be independent:

- illness
- tiredness
- initially easier to have things done by someone else
- lack of confidence
- fear of failure, so would rather not try.

You need to be very supportive, acknowledge the difficulties and then encourage the client to be independent.

CASE STUDY negotiating levels of assistance

Two weeks ago, Jessie fell and broke her hip. She has had an operation but her leg is still very painful. She is now being encouraged to walk each day to strengthen her leg and keep her mobile. The care worker has come to help Jessie walk down the ward to the toilet. 'I can't be bothered to walk today,' Jessie says. 'The physiotherapist has just been and I have had to do all my exercises and I am very tired. Can you get me the commode?'

▷ Why do you think that Jessie does not want to walk today?

▷ Do you think that she should have a walk?

▷ What can you say to encourage Jessie to have a walk?

• • • *Access to everyday facilities*

Being able to get to the shops and choose your own food and clothes is an important part of being independent.

Access to everyday facilities

...You were not able to access everyday facilities?

Discuss how you might feel if you were not able to choose your own clothes or food, go to the pictures or go out with your friends whenever you wanted.

People may not be able to access everyday facilities because they have poor mobility or there is a lack of transport. Help with mobility can be provided by:

- wheelchairs
- support from a carer
- motorised wheelchairs
- mobility buggies.

Help with transport can be provided by:

- specialist taxi services
- specialist minibus transport for people with disabilities (e.g. Dial-a-Ride)
- low-floored buses where the step can be lowered for prams and wheelchairs
- spaces in some train compartments for wheelchairs.

◼◼◼ EVIDENCE ACTIVITY

Access to everyday facilities to promote independence

1 Using your *Yellow Pages* directory or similar, make a list of taxi companies that provide a service for people with mobility difficulties or wheelchair users.

2 Make a list of local stores and supermarkets. Find out which stores provide wheelchairs for customers.

Other factors that make it difficult for people to access public buildings include:

- narrow doors that twin prams and wheelchairs cannot access
- a lack of nappy changing or disabled toilet facilities
- no lifts in some buildings
- high counters at information points
- telephones which are too high to reach from a wheelchair.

New legislation is being implemented to ensure that public buildings provide appropriate facilities for people with disabilities.

WHAT if

Access in public buildings

...*Your parents bring your grandmother to watch your school play?*

Your parents have visited the school hall to make sure that they can get your granny's wheelchair in, and the staff are keeping a special place for her in the front row. At the interval, Granny needs to visit the toilet. The only toilet with a wide door is the staff toilet on the first floor and there is no lift. Your mum has to miss the second half of the performance to take your granny home.

▷ Why do you think that Granny says that she will never come out with the family again?

▷ What effect will this experience have had on Granny's self-esteem?

• • • *Verbal encouragement and praise*

While supporting people to be independent and learn new skills, you need to provide lots of encouragement and praise. You can praise people both verbally and non-verbally. There are many ways of saying 'well done'. For example, you could say, 'Excellent, you are trying hard, that's very good.'

GIVE IT A GO giving praise

List as many ways as you can of giving praise.

The most effective type of verbal praise is called 'shared praise'. This is when you tell other people about a person's achievement. You might tell everyone that Jessie has walked to the end of the corridor using her crutches, or that Johnny has learnt to tie up his shoelaces.

WHAT if

Giving praise

...*Your teacher tells the class that your assignment was the best in the group?*

Why do you feel particularly proud?

Non-verbal praise can be particularly useful when working with children. Smiling, clapping and giving hugs are all important forms of praise.

Independence needs for different groups

An individual's ability to be independent changes throughout his or her lifetime.

• • • *Infants aged 0–2 years*

Newborn babies are completely dependent on the adults who care for them. As they grow, adults should encourage independence. For example, between the ages of 9 and 10 months, babies should be able to hold a spoon.

• • • *Children aged 2–10 years*

Children become more independent as they grow and develop. For example, children should be doing up their own buttons and zips by the time they are 5 years old.

CASE STUDY | independence in childhood

▷ Farhan could not take off his coat when he went to nursery.

▷ Will could not use a knife and fork when he started school.

▷ Jamilla cannot tie her shoelaces at PE time.

1   What might happen to these children?

2   Why is it important that children are encouraged to be independent?

• • • *Adolescents aged 10–18 years*

During adolescence, young people become independent from their parents as they prepare to leave home and start work. This can be a very stressful time that often involves conflict when parents attempt to 'protect' their children as they start to explore adult life and relationships.

CASE STUDY | independence for adolescents

Charlie broke his neck playing rugby when he was 13. He has an electric wheelchair, which he can steer himself, but he has to have help for feeding. He is now 16 years old and has become very frustrated. He is bad tempered and rude to his parents who have been trying to help him decide what to do when he leaves school.

▷ Why do you think that Charlie is so angry?

▷ Make a list of all the things that you think Charlie would want to do at this age that he might not be able to do.

▷ How could you help him?

• • • *Adults*

Many healthy adults are fully independent, physically, emotionally and financially. They may have a partner or children to share their life and a job earning their own money. However, adults may have to cope with difficulties such as illness, redundancy or divorce. At this time they may revert (go backwards) and become dependent either emotionally or financially on other people.

CASE STUDY independence for adults

Charlene is on her own with four children because her husband has been sent to prison. She has not worked since she left school and she owes a lot of money on her credit cards. Two of her children have severe asthma (a chest condition which sometimes makes breathing difficult) and her eldest child has very challenging behaviour. Charlene was not coping so is getting lots of support from the staff at the local Sure Start service.

▷ Why do you think that Charlene is having difficulty being independent at this particular time?

• • • *Senior citizens*

Currently, the official retirement age is 65 years. After retirement, many people enjoy a good period of time when they are totally independent. However, in later years they may find that their joints become stiff and painful, their muscles become weaker, and their hearing and eyesight is not as good as it once was. People may develop conditions such as heart disease, a stroke or Alzheimer's disease (a condition resulting in loss of memory and confusion). This may mean that independence is limited. If this happens, people may need as much care as when they were babies, requiring help with dressing, feeding, mobility and personal care.

⬤⬤⬤ EVIDENCE ACTIVITY

Independence for different groups

Draw a timeline from birth to today and record your independence needs throughout your whole life.

Describe why it is important to be independent.

• • • *People with disabilities (sensory, emotional, physical)*

People with disabilities may be more likely to need additional help to become independent. However, you must not assume that, just because someone has a disability, that he or she automatically needs your help or that everyone with a particular disability needs the same amount of help. You must first find out what a person needs and then offer him or her support.

Disability	Independence needs
Sensory disability Hearing	May need the support of someone who can use sign language. May need hearing aid or aids such as a flashing doorbell.
Sight	May need the support of a guide dog. May need some aids or gadgets in the house such as large numbers on cooker knobs or dials.
Emotional Mental health problems	May need support with aspects of daily living, making relationships or getting out in the community. May need financial support if unable to work.
Physical	May need help with mobility or aspects of daily living such as dressing or feeding.

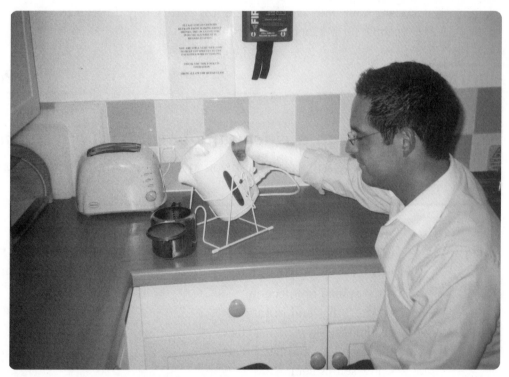

Using a gadget to help with pouring a kettle.

● ● ● *People whose ability is affected by illness, frailty or a developmental stage*

At any stage in life a person may lose his or her independence. This may be caused through illness, which may be of a temporary or permanent nature. For example:

- Lesley has had an operation. She has been told that she cannot drive, carry heavy bags or do heavy housework for six weeks.

- Abdul has broken both legs and will be using a wheelchair and crutches for three or four months.
- Keith has been diagnosed with multiple sclerosis (a progressive condition which may eventually mean that he becomes totally dependent for all aspects of care).

There are many reasons why people are not totally independent. Remember, no two people or conditions are the same and your role is to find out what each person may need and provide that support in a dignified manner.

Supporting personal care

What is meant by personal care?

'Personal care' is the term used to describe care of the body to maintain hygiene, i.e. washing, bathing, dressing or toileting. It is a particularly sensitive type of care. Your body is private and it is particularly difficult to have to rely on other people for personal care.

WHAT if Personal care

...*You have had an accident and burnt both of your hands?*

You need someone to wash you and take you to the toilet. How do you think you would feel?

• • • *Hygiene*

Good hygiene is an important aspect of everyone's life. As a carer you will support clients with a variety of hygiene routines. Poor personal hygiene may result in:

- the spread of infection
- skin rashes and irritations
- gum disease
- body odour and bad breath
- low self-esteem.

WHAT if Personal hygiene

...*a colleague had bad breath and body odour?*

▷ What effect might this have on other members of staff and clients?

▷ What might you do about it?

• • • *Washing*

Washing includes:

- hand washing after toileting and before eating
- cleansing the whole body, particularly the parts where sweat is excreted such as the underarms, groin and feet
- washing your hair and scalp
- cleaning your teeth.

• • • *Dressing*

The term 'dressing' includes choosing what to wear as well as actually putting on the clothes. While some people may just need a little help with doing up buttons or tying shoelaces, other people may need help with all their clothes. Occupational therapists teach people how to dress, and provide aids and gadgets to support dressing.

• • • *Access to toilet facilities*

An accessible toilet should include:

- a wide door to enable a wheelchair or a person walking with carers to pass through
- hand rails to help a client rise from the toilet
- an option to have a raised toilet seat
- a lower basin to make hand washing easy
- a light switch on a cord
- a help alarm so that a client in difficulties can call for help.

The features of an accessible toilet.

• • • **The importance of choice**

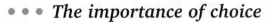

The importance of choice

...*Your mother chose all your clothes and told you what to wear every day?*

How would you feel?

Being able to have a choice and make decisions allows people some control over their lives. This encourages independence and improves self-esteem. People in care settings may lose the ability to make decisions if they do not have regular opportunities to make choices. By, for example, providing craft sessions in a care home where clients choose the items they will make and the materials they will use, clients are helped to make choices in other areas of their lives.

People should be able to choose:

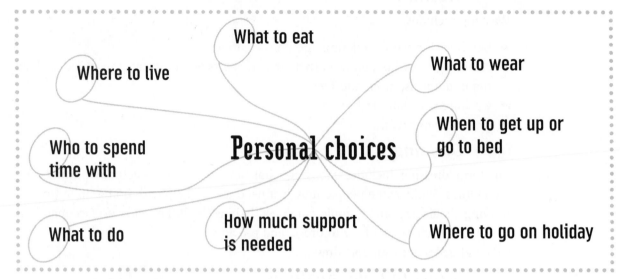

People should be able to choose:

- What to eat
- Where to live
- What to wear
- When to get up or go to bed
- Who to spend time with
- **Personal choices**
- What to do
- How much support is needed
- Where to go on holiday

Skills required for personal care

You have seen that personal care requires a very special approach. Some of the skills that you need are:

- Good communication
- Ability to negotiate
- Sensitivity
- Calm attitude
- **Skills for personal care**
- Polite manner
- Gentle approach
- Understanding of your client and his or her situation
- Ability to take your time

When assisting with personal care:

- Listen carefully to any instructions given to you.
- Introduce yourself to the client and share some brief conversation. This helps the client to feel relaxed and more comfortable in your care.
- Tell the client what you are hoping to do, giving reasons where possible; for example, 'I'm hoping to give you a bath now so that you can have a little rest before tea'.
- Ask the client for permission to carry out this action.

- Ask the client what help is needed.
- Provide the client with as much choice as possible, so that he or she has some control over the situation; for example, what toiletries to use or clothes to wear.
- Talk to the client respectfully throughout, explaining what you are doing and checking on how he or she is feeling.
- Wash your hands carefully before working with an individual client and again at the end of the task.

Hand washing and how to avoid cross-infection

Bacteria grow in warm, damp conditions and can easily be passed from one person to another. It is very important that you are particularly careful about your own personal hygiene, both to protect yourself and the people that you care for.

When washing your hands check that you have:

- used antibacterial soap
- washed your palms
- washed between your fingers and between your thumb and first finger
- rubbed the tips of your fingers, particularly round the nail bed (you may take a nail brush over your nails; always keep your nails clean and short)
- rinsed and dried your hands well.

For more detail, refer to pages 146–147.

Wash hands between clients and after going to the toilet, blowing your nose, coughing or sneezing

Never share towels, hair brushes or toothbrushes

Use disposable gloves when dealing with body waste, blood, urine and faeces

How to avoid cross-infection

Cover all cuts and sores

Dispose of body waste appropriately

Wear a plastic apron to protect your clothes and limit cross-infection

Working in partnership to agree a care approach

Since people often feel uncomfortable when they need help with their personal care, you must ensure the client's needs and wishes are taken into account.

- Ask the client what help is needed.
- Tell the client what help you can give.
- Agree together the amount of support you will give.

 WHAT if   **Working in partnership to provide personal care**

...You were in hospital after an operation on a broken leg?

The care assistant comes over, pulls the screens round the bed and says, 'Good morning, it's bath time.' She takes off your night clothes and starts to wash your body. She uses a different cloth for your groin area. While washing you she talks cheerfully telling you about her recent holiday.

📓 Describe how you might feel.

📓 What would you have preferred her to do?

••• How to demonstrate respect for individual choice

You can demonstrate respect for individual choice by:

- offering opportunities to make decisions and have a choice
- encouraging people to make decisions
- being polite and respectful
- concealing your own opinion in order to agree with a client
- giving praise for decisions made.

 **WHAT if**   **Respect for individual choice**

...You are a carer at Meadowsweet Care Home?

What would you say in the following situations?

📓 Mrs Lightfoot is getting dressed for the Christmas party. She wants to wear a red dress with an orange cardigan so that she will look nice and bright for all her visitors. You think that the colours clash and that she looks very silly.

📓 You are bathing Mr Welford. He has said that he does not want you to use that 'horrible smelly soap that makes him smell like a hairdressers'. You like the soap.

📓 You have gone on a home visit with Mrs Hobbes before she is discharged from hospital. You think that the house is dirty, smelly and overcrowded. The carpet is rather sticky and the chairs look greasy. Mrs Hobbes is very excited at being home and is longing to show you all her possessions. 'Sit down now dearie, and let me show you all the pictures of my family.' You are not keen to sit on the grubby chair.

• • • *How to maintain privacy and dignity*

All clients have a right to privacy and dignity, and it is important that you respect this right.

- Always use a client's preferred name.
- Ask permission before undertaking any care routine.
- Check that doors are closed or curtains pulled round during personal care routines.
- Only discuss personal matters in private.
- If a client becomes distressed take him or her into a private area.
- Clients should be able to see visitors or make phone calls in private.

CASE STUDY maintaining privacy and dignity

You are working at Meadowsweet Nursing Home. Yesterday, Lucy came into the lounge to speak to Mrs Florrie Lightfoot. 'Now Florrie, it appears you have got a bit of infection in your wound. The doctor has come to see you, but I am in a hurry so he will look at it in here.' When Lucy and the doctor finished with Mrs Lightfoot (who does not like being called Florrie), you told Lucy that Mr Waterfoot's urine bag was full. 'Oh bother,' said Lucy, 'I'm very late.' She rushed off and collected a new bag and changed it in the lounge where all the other clients could see.

▷ Describe the mistakes that Lucy made.

▷ What would you have done if you had been in charge?

⬛⬛⬤ EVIDENCE ACTIVITY

What do you understand to be personal care?

Your cousin is at college learning to be an electrician. He has sent you an email about what he has learnt this term on his course. Write an email or letter back to him describing, in simple and clear terms, what is meant by personal care.

Keep the email or letter safely in your file.

Assisting with mobility

Many people in care settings need help to move around.

• • • *Regulations around lifting and handling*

The Manual Handling Operations Regulations, which came into force in January 1993, and the Health and Safety at Work Act 1974 provide clear guidelines for safe practices. The law states that both employers and employees have specific responsibilities in relation to safety. Employers must:

- ensure that staff do not undertake any lifting that may cause an injury (this can mean lifting clients, goods or equipment)
- make an assessment of the manual handling or lifting situation
- take action to reduce the risk of injury.

Employers must make a full risk assessment of any lifting situation for all clients in the setting. They will assess whether lifting is really required or whether special equipment can be used. They will assess the weight of the person to be lifted, how mobile he or she is and what help can be provided. They will also assess the experience and training of the employee responsible for lifting.

Employees also have responsibilities under the law. They must:

- keep themselves safe and avoid lifting
- keep the clients safe
- follow all safety procedures.

All care settings will have a policy on manual lifting and handling which tells staff what they are expected to do.

••• *Reasons for the regulations*

Injuries caused by poor lifting techniques mean that people take time off work and may develop long-term health problems. Poor lifting practices can also cause injury to clients. As an example, if you lift a client from his or her chair while supporting him or her under the arms, this can cause injury to the client's shoulders.

Staff in care settings have regular lifting and handling training. **You should never attempt to move or lift another person without appropriate training.**

••• *Managing moving and lifting*

Staff often use aids to help lift and move clients. These include hoists (to lift a whole body), sliding boards (where the client can slide along a board between bed and chair) or swivel boards (which a client can stand on to transfer from a bed to a chair). However, as with lifting, you must have special training before using any of these aids.

The most important aspect when managing moving and lifting is to encourage the client to provide as much assistance as possible. You can do this by:

- telling the client what you are going to do
- gaining his or her co-operation
- asking him or her what help he or she can give
- giving him or her advice about what he or she can do to help
- providing praise and encouragement throughout the process.

To promote independence always remember the saying: 'You will be working *with* a client rather than *for* a client.'

GIVE IT A GO lifting and handling

Bessie is 97 years old. The manager of the home has asked you to help Carol to put Bessie to bed. Carol tells you that she is going on her break and asks if you can put Bessie to bed on your own. 'She doesn't need much help – I am sure you will manage,' Carol says.

▷ What are you going to do?

▷ What might happen if you try to put Bessie to bed on your own?

unit 4

Personal effectiveness

This unit is designed to give you the opportunity to find out about yourself. In this busy world it can be difficult to find the time to 'reflect' (think about) ourselves: the skills and knowledge we already have and those we would like to develop. Unless you take the time to think about your future, planning and preparing can be difficult. Once you know the kind of work that you would like to do, you can prepare yourself and gather the qualifications that you need to be successful.

This unit offers you the opportunity to prepare for work in the health, social care and early years sectors.

In this unit you will learn about:

▷ carrying out a personal audit of your skills and knowledge

▷ making an assessment of your potential

▷ matching your skills and knowledge to a range of jobs

▷ completing a curriculum vitae (CV) and preparing a personal statement and portfolio for a prospective employer.

Personal audit of skills and knowledge

A personal audit can be exciting to complete, especially if you carry out the tasks involved as honestly and truthfully as you can. There is no point pretending or writing false information about yourself because you would only be 'fooling yourself'. A personal audit is for your own use, no one else's. It allows you to reflect and think about who you are and what you want to do with your life (certainly at this point). A personal audit is not a 'one off' activity. It is something that needs to be carried out regularly, perhaps even yearly. As you develop your skills and knowledge, so your personal audit results change.

A personal audit needs to be carried out in a systematic and organised way, and should always include the following:

- your vocational skills
- your personal skills
- your interpersonal (social) skills
- your behaviour
- your interests.

Vocational skills

When something is referred to as 'vocational' it usually means that it is related to work for which a person is particularly suited. In the health, social care and early years sectors, we often refer to people as 'having a vocation'. In this sense, your personal skills audit needs to begin with you thinking about the skills you have that are related to the kind of work you are interested in.

● ● ● *Work-related experiences*

Think about your work experience up to now. This includes work that is part-time, whether paid or unpaid (including 'voluntary' work and work experience). It may be that you have not worked in health, social care or early years before, but that should not matter. Examples of work that you have done could include:

- babysitting for friends or relatives
- working in a shop
- working on a market stall
- a newspaper round
- working in a café or restaurant
- helping older people with their shopping
- taking people out for the day.

GIVE IT A GO — work experience

Use the chart to help you think about the kind of work that you have done in the past. You will probably find that you can fill in many of the columns. A couple of examples have been done for you.

Work I have done	Full-time or part-time	Paid work	Voluntary work	Work experience
Worked in a chip shop	Part-time (3 hours per week)	Yes		
Looked after my sister on a Saturday		No	Yes	

Once you have completed this chart you will be able to think about the skills and knowledge you have gained as a result of your experiences.

• • • Skills and knowledge

You may be thinking that you have not learned anything from your work. In reality, however, you will have learned a great deal. You will need to think about that learning to help you complete your personal audit.

GIVE IT A GO — learning and skills development

Answer the following questions to help you identify the learning that has taken place as a result of your work experiences.

- Did the work involve being with people?
- Did the work involve children?
- Did the work involve older people?
- Was handling money part of the work?
- Did you have to be there 'on time'?
- Did the work require you to be organised?

If you answered 'yes' to any of these questions, you will need to think about your learning and skills development around 'meeting the needs of other people'. For example, customer service is a great skill to have.

• • • *Qualifications*

Once you have identified your work experiences and skills development, it is a good idea to think about the qualifications that you already have. Again, you will need to think about this in a broad way – don't just think about the qualifications that you gained at school (although these should be included). Think about other qualifications that you might have gained as a result of work or hobbies.

For example, many people join the St John Ambulance Brigade out of an interest as well as a desire to help others. Perhaps you gained a certificate in this way? Perhaps you gained a first aid certificate or a food hygiene certificate as part of your job or as part of another qualification? It is important to remember the qualifications that you have achieved as part of your daily life. Other examples of qualifications that you might have achieved could include:

- swimming certificates
- dance certificates
- certificates for piano or other musical instruments
- gym certificates
- Duke of Edinburgh award(s)
- driving licence.

GIVE IT A GO | listing qualifications

Make a list of all the qualifications that you have achieved. Don't dismiss any as 'not relevant'. Make sure you write them all down. Keep the list in a safe place as you will need it later.

Personal skills

Personal skills are those which relate to you as an individual. They may be some of the qualities that your friends would use to describe you. When we look at personal skills there are three main things to take account of:

- appearance
- posture
- body language.

• • • *Appearance*

We all have a particular dress code that we like to follow, whether being in the height of fashion or being smart and wearing suits. Whatever your dress code, you should be aware of your appearance and the image it gives to others.

Appearance

...You were to ask other people to comment on your appearance?

What do you think they would say?

• • • *Uniform*

Working in health, social care and early years demands a clean, neat and hygienic appearance. Clothes are used to inspire confidence in clients. If you look dirty and uncared for then it can be assumed that you are unlikely to care for others very well. In most care places, staff are asked to wear a uniform so that clients can easily identify the carers. A uniform also helps to protect your clothes and, to some extent, prevent cross-infection.

CASE STUDY considering your appearance

Diane has been asked by her supervisor at work to look at herself and describe her dress code. Her supervisor explained that she meant her appearance as it usually is. Diane looked at her clothes. 'Casual', she thought. Big, baggy jumper, food stains on the front. Denim jeans (one size too small) with the bottom frayed on one leg, and dirty, white trainers with odd laces. 'Scruffy' she though to herself, 'not casual'.

How would you describe Diane's appearance? What do you think her supervisor is thinking? After all, Diane is working in a care home, looking after older people.

• • • *Posture and body language*

'Body language' is the term used to describe the things we are saying or thinking without using words. Posture is part of body language and can say a great deal about you. Try the 'Give it a go' activities on the next page.

Interpersonal skills

These are the skills that you use every day with other people. They are the techniques that you use to make people like you or to make people leave you alone. In health, social care and early years work, your interpersonal skills are extremely important. Developing good relationships with your clients is important. You need to develop trust and honesty as part of the caring process. It is your interpersonal skills that will help you to develop these good relationships.

GIVE IT A GO — using body language

Look at the faces and decide which one is sad, happy or angry.

It is easy to see which face is which because we are used to reading the body language of other people.

GIVE IT A GO — posture

Which of these people sitting at the desk is:

☐ interested

☐ bored

☐ asleep?

Now think about your body language and posture. What messages are you giving to other people?

Interpersonal skills need to be built around the care value base (see also pages 63–65). This means that our starting point for all interactions (talking or being with other people) is built on:

- respect
- choice
- dignity
- equal opportunity
- professionalism
- confidentiality.

By following the care value base, you should be able to 'get on with other people'. Showing respect for others is a good way of getting them to respect you back. If you are professional in everything you do, your working relationships should be good.

GIVE IT A GO · the care value base

Look at the list of words on page 111 that are related to the care value base and think about how you relate to other people. Do you show respect? Do you behave in a professional manner? Are you good at keeping confidences?

You will need to include your interpersonal skills in your personal audit, so make notes about how you think you relate to others.

Behaviour

'Behaviour' means the way we respond to certain situations and people. For example, if you were late for an appointment, would you shout and scream at the people around you? If the answer is yes, then we could say that your behaviour is unacceptable in that situation. After all, the lateness is your responsibility!

● ● ● *Expected behaviour*

In health, social care and early years work, there is an expected form of behaviour. Once again, this relates to the care value base and includes behaviour patterns that are:

- professional
- calm
- polite
- show a willingness to listen
- show a willingness to learn
- designed to keep information confidential
- caring
- empathic
- well organised
- punctual (always on time).

CASE STUDY · appropriate behaviour

Karen has been told that she must begin to 'smarten up' her appearance when she is at work. She has a job caring for older people in a nursing home and is rather slapdash in her habits. Last week she was caught wearing too much jewellery: she had a ring on every finger, studs in her ears, nose and tongue, and half a dozen chains around her neck. Her clothes are never clean. She has a uniform but seems to wear it until it is totally unhygienic. Now her manager has had enough. She says Karen must make an effort or she will be out of work.

CASE STUDY appropriate behaviour continued

Karen has 'slammed' out of the nurse's office and is shouting at her colleagues in the tea room. She has told them that she doesn't care who hears her! She says that she is not going to do any more work until 'that woman' apologises.

▷ Describe Karen's behaviour. Is it what you would expect from someone who has the responsibility for the care of others? How might Karen's clients react?

▷ Working with another student, reread the case study and discuss the things you think Karen needs to change in both her behaviour and appearance.

If Karen is going to learn how to become a professional member of the team she needs to:

- learn to listen
- be ready to accept justified criticism
- learn not to take her frustration out on her colleagues
- be ready to put the needs of her clients first
- develop a more professional attitude.

But just how easy is it to modify (change) your behaviour?

 **WHAT if** **Modifying behaviour**

...You have promised yourself that you are going to change?

It might be that you have said that you will take up more exercise, go on a healthy eating plan, or do your homework on time. Did you manage to change your behaviour?

Changing our behaviour is not easy but it certainly is not impossible. It all comes down to wanting to change and a willingness to listen and learn. Karen could change her behaviour if she truly wants to. She has people all around her who would be only too willing to help her make the changes.

In order to change we have to:

- decide on the new behaviours that we want to develop
- be realistic (not expecting too many changes at once)
- set achievable targets (it's no good trying to change the impossible)
- look for people who can help us
- ask for help.

Once we know what needs changing and how we can make a difference to our behaviour, we can begin to make the changes. Then we will need to practise the new behaviours over and over again until they become a habit and are a normal way for us to behave.

Interests

When carrying out a personal audit, we also need to include our personal interests (sometimes called 'hobbies'). You might enjoy working with people or animals, or enjoy gardening or drawing. Whichever of these you like doing, you will need to think about the skills and knowledge you have gained through participating in the activities. For example, if you work with animals you will learn to care for them, clean up after them, train them, and learn about their needs and habits. All of these knowledge and skills are going to prove useful if you choose to work in the health, social care and early years sectors.

 **EVIDENCE ACTIVITY**

Personal audit and suitable jobs

Using all your notes and the work you have completed as part of this unit, carry out a personal audit to identify your work-related skills. You might like to use a chart such as the one you completed on page 108.

Then, looking back at the evidence activity from Unit 1 (page 38) in your portfolio:
(a) decide if the list of suitable 'jobs' that interested you needs to be changed
(b) draw up a new list and give brief reasons for any changes
(c) if there are no changes, explain why.

Assessing your potential

When we talk about someone's potential, we are talking about his or her future – what *could* be. The potential might be high, i.e. it could be that someone is destined to become a doctor or nurse. A person's potential could also be about working with other people, earning a great deal of money or something entirely different.

This part of the unit asks you to think about your own potential:

- What might you become?
- What are you capable of?
- What do you like or dislike?

Assessment

In order to examine your potential, you need to make another assessment of yourself by finding out about your strengths and weaknesses, and suitable job choices.

There are two ways to find out about your strengths and weaknesses. These are through:

- self-assessment
- assessment by others.

When we talked earlier about reflection and thinking over our skills, we were 'self-assessing'. When somebody else, for example, our manager or supervisor, tells us about our strengths or skills, it is 'assessment by others'.

CASE STUDY post-appraisal thoughts

Abdul has just had his appraisal and is thinking about some of the discussions he has had with his manager. His manager said that his strengths lie in caring for other people, being a team worker and being well-organised. Abdul is pleased about this feedback but wonders if his strengths ought to include his willingness to learn about his new job. His manager never mentioned that quality and Abdul knows he works hard at his studies. He really wants to qualify as a nurse one day.

▷ What kind of assessment has Abdul taken part in? Is there more than one kind of assessment in this example?

In order to carry out an assessment of your potential, you need to have a good idea about your strengths and weaknesses. You already know about the care value base (see pages 63–65), so it might be a good idea to think about the strengths required to work in health, social care and early years before you start.

GIVE IT A GO qualities required for caring

Working with another person, make a list of the qualities required by someone who cares for children. Then make a list for someone who cares for older people. Some of the qualities will be the same, so you can merge the two lists into one when you have finished.

It is likely that the strengths you have identified are:

- ability to listen
- ability to ask appropriate questions
- confident approach
- good time keeping
- ability to get on with other people
- ability to follow instructions
- good administrative skills

- ability to use initiative
- ability to learn new skills
- ability to work as part of a team.

• • • *Ability to follow instructions*

Following instructions is 'doing as you are told' when asked by someone in authority. There is no room for mistakes here: in health, social care and early years you are not working with objects; you are working with people and are responsible for their care needs.

• • • *Good administrative skills*

In all kinds of care there is paperwork to be completed. This can include filling in or filing patient records, making appointments, taking messages or ordering stock. It requires someone who:

- pays attention to detail
- can be trusted
- can write and understand numbers
- can file in order.

• • • *Using your initiative*

This means being able to think for yourself. Again, in health, social care and early years work it is important that you are able to do this. However, being able to use your initiative does not mean making decisions about a client's care or his or her needs. It means checking out with someone senior that what you think needs to be done is the right thing for that individual.

CASE STUDY) when initiative can go wrong

Milly is a new care worker on Ward 11. One of the patients is waiting to go to theatre for an operation. He is desperate for a drink of water. He calls to Milly who says she will get him one. She decides not to bother the staff nurse who is very busy with another patient, and gives him a large glass of water which he drinks gratefully.

Milly tells staff nurse what she has done when she has finished with the other patient. 'Oh no,' says the staff nurse, 'We will have to cancel his operation as he should have been nil by mouth.'

▷ What has happened in this case with Milly using her initiative? What harm has it done to her client?

• • • *Learning new skills*

Having the ability and the willingness to learn new skills is essential in health, social care and early years work. This is not only important as you start your career but continues to be important as your career develops. In health, social care and early years, new ways of working are constantly being discovered or recommended. People employed in this sector have got to be flexible and able to learn new skills to 'keep up with the job'.

GIVE IT A GO   your strengths

Discuss with another person those things that you think are strengths about yourself. Think about some of the compliments you have had, either from your manager, your course tutor or the people you live with. You could even include compliments given by your friends (if they relate to the strengths in the care value base).

• • • *Ability to work as part of a team*

If you are unable to work in a team, this is a serious weakness and one that would need to be addressed if you are to work in the health, social care and early years sectors.

CASE STUDY   what type of job?

1   Tuesday morning is the time of Clare's team meeting. She hates these meetings as she feels that the rest of the team 'pick on her'. From start to finish she feels as though her work is being criticised. She has already been told that her team work skills are poor and that she does not seem to understand the importance of finishing off a job properly. 'I can't see why it matters,' she thinks to herself, 'someone else will do it if I don't. It's not as if the clients are affected!'

2   Swami is dreading today's team meeting. He knows that Clare's inability to work as part of the team is going to cause a problem again. He has already explained how Clare never finishing tasks affects the rest of her team. Audrey has made it clear that if she comes to work to find that all the clients' washing and ironing is waiting for her again, when it is not her turn, she will explode. Mary is still feeling angry at having to help Albert finish his meal, two hours after it was given to him. Albert should not be left needing help at any time but especially when Clare was asked to support him through his evening meal. 'It's just not good enough! What am I going to do?' thought Swami.

▷   Discuss with another person Clare's attitude towards her work and the way it is making her team members feel.

▷   Is client care affected by Clare's attitude? How would you feel if you had to work alongside Clare?

Clare is unable to contribute towards team working effectively. She does not demonstrate any of the qualities needed by a team member:

- professionalism
- caring
- supporting
- trustworthiness
- commitment.

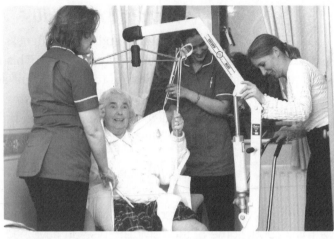

Working as part of a team.

These are just five examples of what is wanted from a good team member. If you are unable to demonstrate these qualities when you are working as part of a team, your potential for health, social care and early years work is going to be very limited.

GIVE IT A GO   team work skills

Think about any tasks or activities that you have undertaken as part of a team. How did you do? How did others contribute to the team work? How would you describe yourself as a team member?

Give yourself a score:

1 = Excellent   **2** = Very good   **3** = Fair   **4** = Not very good   **5** = Poor

Now ask someone else who has worked with you in a team to score your contribution. Do the scores match?

Matching skills and knowledge to jobs

In this section you will find out more about different job roles in the health, social care and early years sectors. At the same time you will be able to see if your strengths suit one job better than they do other jobs.

In order to match your strengths to job roles, you are asked to use a job description and a person specification. Therefore, you need to understand the purpose of these documents and how to obtain them.

Job descriptions

A job description is written by employers to tell others about a job vacancy in their organisation. The job description describes what the job is all about and includes:

- the job title
- the salary or rate of pay
- the main task(s) to be carried out
- who the line manager is
- where the job is based
- how many hours are to be worked in a week.

In addition, the main parts of the job are broken down into a series of tasks, actions and knowledge requirements. These help you to decide if you are interested in the job and whether you would be able to do the job well.

ANYTOWN NHS HOSPITAL TRUST

ANYTOWN HOSPITAL

Job Description

Job title: F/T Health Care Assistant
Salary grade: Grade A or equivalent
Department: Infectious Diseases Unit
Accountable to: Staff Nurse

Purpose

1   To assist nursing staff with direct patient care.

2   To keep the ward environment tidy and well maintained.

3   To provide administrative/technical/clerical support to the nursing team which will contribute to the efficiency and smooth running of the ward.

Specific responsibilities

Patient Care

1   To assist qualified nurses with the care of patients.

2   To carry out the following aspects of patient care under the direction and supervision of a registered nurse:

providing reassurance and comfort by establishing good relationships with the patients, family and friends whilst maintaining their dignity, privacy and confidence at all times, including social 'chat', especially for isolated patients

maintenance of patients' hygiene, including bathing of the patients in bed or in the bathroom, care of skin, hair, mouth, eyes, hand and feet, care of clothing and assisting dressing

minimising the risk of pressure sores by relief of pressure through assisting the patient to change position or the use of mechanical aids or appliances

positioning of patients who are unable to help themselves by using the appropriate lifting and handling techniques, including the use of mechanical aids

helping with elimination needs by giving and removing bedpans, urinals and commodes, assisting patients to walk to the toilet, assisting with the care of incontinent patients and recording urine output and bowel scan

assisting with nutrition by helping patients into a comfortable position at meal and beverage times, feeding patients by mouth as needed, making drinks and snacks to supplement patients' diets, helping patients choose from the daily menu, recording fluid and food intake and distributing and collecting menus

assisting with the care of the dying and last offices

observing the patient's condition and anxieties and reporting information to the nursing team, including formal observations of temperature, pulse and respiration

escorting patients within the hospital area when no nursing needs are identified which require a registered nurse.

Ward Environment

To keep patient lockers and other furniture surfaces in the ward clean and tidy

to keep the relatives' kitchen and bedroom clean and tidy

to be responsible for general bed-making, including stripping, cleaning and remaking beds of discharged patients, and preparing for the admission of new patients

to keep the ward storage areas clean, tidy and appropriately stocked

to check, clean and store equipment, ensuring faulty equipment is reported

to be aware of and comply with the relevant Trust, Clinical Centre and SDU policies

to assist with relocating patients and their belongings within the ward area.

Support for the Nursing team

To answer the telephone and take messages when the ward clerk is not available

to be available to collect and deliver ward equipment and pharmacy within the hospital as necessary

to undertake specific administrative tasks as delegated by the qualified staff, including ordering of patients' transport

to contribute to the life and development of the ward, including the maintenance of a good working atmosphere.

Personal Development

To be aware of own limitations and seek assistance and guidance of a qualified nurse as appropriate

to participate in review of performance with the SDU Manager/Team Leader and negotiate development opportunities

to keep up to date with statutory study days.

To adhere to Anytown Hospital NHS Trust policies with regard to:

Minimal Manual Handling
Infection Control
COSHH
Fire and Accidents
Patients' Property.

Personal specification

This is another piece of information that is provided by the employer. It states exactly what skills and qualifications are required by the job. These are often put under two headings:

- essential
- desirable.

If the skill or qualification is 'essential', you must have it in order to be offered an interview. Therefore, if you cannot match your skills and qualifications to 'essential criteria' (standards) there is no point in applying for the job. But remember, there is nothing stopping you from collecting essential criteria through extra study or voluntary work.

'Desirable' criteria are those things that employers would like you to have. However, if you don't have them they may still be willing to interview you, as long as all the essential criteria are met.

PERSON SPECIFICATION
Health Care Assistant

The Employee	Essential	Desirable
Physical attributes	Good attendance record Neat and tidy appearance	
Education/Qualifications	General level of education	Potential to complete NVQ Level 2 Foundation GNVQ Health and Social Care
Previous experience		Some experience of caring in any setting
Personal characteristics	Positive and enthusiastic Friendly personality Hard working Reliable and punctual Flexible and adaptable Non-judgmental Good sense of humour	
Special aptitudes	Good communication skills – written and verbal Willing to learn Willing to accept constructive criticism Ability to organise own work load Ability to work within a team Aware of own limitations Tolerance of other's limitations Good telephone manner	

CASE STUDY job hunting

Rowan has seen a job he is interested in. He would like to be a classroom assistant and help the teacher with young children's reading and writing needs. He has sent for the details of the job and is now looking at the 'person specification'. He has never seen one before. 'Wow, this is helpful, I can see exactly what skills and knowledge the employer needs. It looks to me like I could do this job. I think I will send in an application'.

Person Specification – Teaching Assistant

Knowledge

A good understanding of child development.
A sound understanding of how young children learn.
An understanding of school systems and structures.

Skills

A teaching assistant qualification or substantial experience as a volunteer.
Able to read easily.
Good with numbers.

Experience

Of working with children in a teaching or similar environment.
Of supporting teachers or others in a voluntary or employed capacity.

When Rowan looked at the person specification he recognised some of his own experiences. He used to help out at a 'Dads and Lads' session. He supported the teacher who was trying to help fathers and their children to develop their reading, writing and maths skills.

Working with others, discuss the skills and knowledge Rowan requires for the job. Would you agree that he should apply for the post? Why?

Developing an action plan

Developing an action plan will help you to put into place the steps you need to take to fulfil your potential. An action plan is easy to produce but for it to be useful it needs to contain key information:

- goals and targets
- timescales
- personal development needs
- work-related development needs.

▣▣▣▣ EVIDENCE ACTIVITY

Matching up to requirements

Working with another person, look for job adverts in your local newspaper. Once you have found one or two that interest you, send for the details so that you have a 'live' job description to work from.

When you receive the information, look at your list of personal strengths and compare them with the job description and person specification. Then complete the 'know yourself' test.

Statements	Not at all	Sometimes	Very much
I like to keep written records			
I enjoy working outside			
I like to meet new people			
I enjoy working in a team			
I like to help people and give advice			
I enjoy using my practical skills			
I like to travel from place to place			
I prefer to work alone most of the time			
I like to have some responsibility			
I try to look neat and tidy all the time			
I prefer to work in the same place/building every day			
I can cope well with emotional situations			
I like working with children			
I like working with people who need additional support			
I enjoy being involved with physical tasks			
I like working with older people			
I would not mind working shifts and at weekends			

Do the answers to the 'know yourself' test indicate that you would be a suitable person for any of the jobs being advertised? Make notes of the ways you would match the requirements and keep these in your folder.

• • • *Goals and targets*

Goals and targets are the things that you want to achieve – some people call them targets and some people call them goals. Here we will call them goals for simplicity.

When you are developing your action plan, you need to think about the goals you want to achieve. An example of a goal could be:

- wanting to finish a qualification
- wanting to start a qualification
- learning how to work in a team
- knowing how to write a CV.

A goal can be anything that you want it to be. However, for a goal to be useful it has to be SMART:

Specific – the goal needs to say exactly what you mean.
Measurable – you must be able to tell when you have achieved your goal.
Achievable – you need to make sure that the goals that you set can be achieved.
Realistic – you need to make sure that the goal can be done taking other things into account, e.g. the time you have available.
Timely – you need to aim to achieve your goal at the right time and over the right time span.

GIVE IT A GO reviewing your strengths and weaknesses

1   Think about your strengths and weaknesses. Have another look at the lists you have made. Remind yourself of the information that you included in your personal audit and then make notes of the things you would like to develop in yourself.

2   Now make two lists, one with the heading 'personal development' and one with the heading 'work-based development'. Use the table below to help you.

Development needs	Qualifications	Skills	Qualities	Knowledge
Personal development		Learning to get on well with everyone	Being cheerful, being positive	Understanding myself better
Work-based development	First aid certificate, Food hygiene certificate	Helping children settle in on their first day at nursery	Being reliable, being trustworthy	How to treat minor accidents in children

3   Use IT to produce a table like the one shown here and then fill it in. Keep it in a safe place because you will need it later.

• • • *Personal and work-based development*

It is likely that by now you have had the chance to really reflect upon your skills and knowledge. You have a good idea of the things you are strong at and a good idea of those things that you need to develop further. The 'content' of your action plan is now taking shape.

Evaluation

Evaluation is taking time to reflect on your goals and achievements. Some people only evaluate at the end of the time agreed; others evaluate sections of their action plan. It might be helpful to think of evaluation as 'examining the successful achievement (or not, as the case may be) of the goals you have set'. Some questions that will help you to evaluate your action plan are:

- Did I reach my goals?
- Did I need more information to help me?
- What are the improvements in my personal and professional life?
- What new knowledge have I gained?
- What new skills have I gained?
- How am I different as a result of the work I have undertaken?

Monitoring and review

Monitoring is a way of checking your action plan to see how it is progressing. Once you have identified the action to achieve your goals, you need to make sure that you are on track to achieve them. If you have set goals that will take a whole year to achieve and you don't track your progress, you could find you never get there! Reviewing your action plan offers you the opportunity to make changes to the plan if you think they are needed.

CASE STUDY · reviewing an action plan

Andy has written his action plan for his personal and professional development. He included as one of his goals his wish to learn a second language. He has chosen Spanish because he thinks it might be helpful to his work. Now he finds that he is going to move to another area that has a large population of Hindi speakers. He decides to change his action plan to reflect this and goes to his local college to see if there are any classes available in Hindi.

How easy do you think it will be to make changes to your action plan? You will need to think about the different stages of your action plan, for example, beginning, middle or near the end.

⬛⬛⬜ EVIDENCE ACTIVITY

Preparing and developing your action plan

Use your answers to the 'know yourself' test on page 122 to start an action plan.

Action plan

I have the following strengths:

_____

_____

I have the following skills:

_____

_____

I have the following qualifications and achievements:

_____

_____

I should like to end up working as:

_____

To achieve my goals I need to:

_____

_____

_____

I need training in the following areas:

_____

_____

I need personal development in the following areas:

_____

_____

I need work experience in the following areas:

_____

_____

My short-term goals are:

_____

_____

My long-term goals are:

_____

_____

Now that you have collected a great deal of information about yourself, you can make a start on developing an action plan to develop your strengths and reduce your weaknesses. You could use IT to produce one like this:

Action plan to develop strengths and weaknesses

Goals and targets	Training needed	Qualifications required	Date to start	Date for completion	Monitoring dates	Date for evaluation
Improve my appearance	Clothes care	None	Today, 8 Sept	30 Sept	15 Sept	30 Sept
Gain a Level 1 qualification						
Develop better time-keeping skills						

CV, personal statement and portfolio

Curriculum Vitae [CV]

A CV is a written statement that tells an employer your life history as it relates to gaining employment. This is the document that employers generally ask for when people apply for jobs. Writing a CV gives you the chance to show your experience and tell an employer what you are capable of. In addition, it allows you to demonstrate your written skills, IT skills and organisational skills (writing in a logical sequence). A CV also enables you to give your contact details to an employer.

A CV should be:

- short
- to the point
- comprehensive (includes all relevant information)
- accurate
- clear
- truthful
- inspiring
- make the employer want to know more about you.

GIVE IT A GO   writing a CV

Use the following headings to help you write a curriculum vitae:

▷ **Name and address** – the information that will enable an employer to contact you. You might want to include your telephone number(s) and email address(es).

▷ **Education and qualifications** (your time at school) – give the dates when you achieved your qualifications, with the most recent first. Don't forget to say where you studied for the qualification.

▷ **Additional training and awards achieved** – include any other training or awards you have achieved that are related to the job you are interested in or to the care sector in general.

▷ **Employment history** (don't forget work experience and part-time jobs) – give the dates, again the most recent first.

▷ **Personal achievements** – these could be the things that you are proud of achieving but don't relate directly to the job role. They will help to give the employer an all-round picture of you.

▷ **Interests** – putting your interests on the CV also helps to show an employer what you are really like. We can often tell a great deal about a person from the things they like to do.

A personal statement

While the CV contains most of the facts relating to your job application, a personal statement gives you the chance to explain to an employer why you want a particular job and why you think that you are the right person for the job. Some employers do not request personal statements but if you are asked to send in a letter of application with your CV, you can include your personal statement as part of the letter. At interview, you can use your personal statement when you explain why you want the job and think that you are the best candidate.

Portfolio

You may be asked to prepare a portfolio that contains the following information and evidence of your skills and knowledge:

- evidence of your telephone ability
- completed job application forms
- letters of application and acceptance
- evidence of your preparation for interviews
- evidence of practice interviews.

• • • *Telephone evidence*

Using a telephone for work is not an easy task. There are many differences between using a telephone for recreation and using one for work.

GIVE IT A GO | telephone evidence

Working with another student, add to the list of the differences between using the phone with friends and using the phone for work.

Work	**Friends**
☐ Speak clearly	☐ Might use slang
☐ Sound interested	☐ Could indicate boredom
☐ Be polite	☐ Want to 'have a laugh'
☐ Check for understanding	☐ Could tell jokes or be personal
☐ Speedy	☐ May not be responsive
☐ Responsive	☐ Could waste time

Your portfolio has to show evidence that you can use the telephone in a professional and polite manner. When working in health, social care and early years, it is very important that you are able to put people at ease when they are speaking to you, whether by phone or face to face. People who are ill or frightened can struggle to make themselves understood or to understand what is being said to them. That is why you should be able to check for understanding.

• • • *Ways of checking for understanding*

- Ask the client if he or she understands (without being rude).
- Paraphrase the client's information back to the client (repeat the information to make sure you have heard right).
- At the end of the conversation, 'sum up' what has been said.

GIVE IT A GO | telephone role play

In pairs, role-play a conversation in which a client phones a receptionist to ask to make an appointment for visiting her doctor. You need to:

☐ decide who is the receptionist and who is the client

☐ both spend a few minutes planning your conversations.

After acting out the role play, change roles before discussing how easy or hard the task was.

Once you are confident at using the telephone, you could ask your tutor to observe you in a staged role play (one that the tutor has planned) so that you can put your tutor's witness statement about your skills and ability on the telephone in your portfolio.

• • • *Completed application forms*

There is only one way to include these in your portfolio and that is to obtain some application forms from employers. Start by looking for suitable jobs in the local press, then send for the application forms and fill them in. You will need to make sure that you:

- complete all the relevant sections
- use the correct coloured pen
- write clearly
- spell everything correctly
- answer truthfully
- provide accurate information
- keep the form clean and tidy.

• • • *Letter of application*

Employers often ask for a letter of application to be sent along with a CV. This letter should be used to support your job application. For example, you can say why you think you would be the best person for the job (as in a personal statement). The letter of application also provides the employer with extra information about you, for example, your handwriting or word-processing skills.

A good letter of application will contain some or all of the following:

- personal details, name, address and telephone number
- job title or reference number
- reference to the enclosed CV or application form
- an indication of your interest in the job and brief reasons as to why you think you are suitable for it
- answers to any particular questions the employer may have asked
- an indication of when you are available for interview
- any times you are not available for interview (e.g. when you are sitting exams).

⬛⬛⬛ EVIDENCE ACTIVITY

Letter of application and personal statement

Using the job advert details that you obtained earlier, select one job that you would like to apply for. First, you need to hand write a letter to the organisation asking that you are considered for the job. Second, you need to produce another (or the same) letter using IT. You can have several practices at this task before you choose a letter for your portfolio. Finally, you need to write a personal statement (no more than 200 words) which will make the employer want to interview *you* for the job.

Ask your tutor to check the work you have done before adding it to your portfolio of evidence.

• • • *Preparation and practice for interviews*

The interview is the part of the job application process that worries people the most, including the people doing the interviewing! The interview is designed so that the best person for the job is chosen. It is therefore a good idea to practise an interview before the 'real thing', and to treat the practice as though it were real.

Before the interview

- Find out as much as possible about the job.

- Look back at your application form and CV and try to imagine the questions that you will be asked about them.

- Refresh your memory about the skills and knowledge that the job requires.

- Talk to experienced or qualified people in similar jobs.

Going to the interview

Appearance is important; avoid:

- wearing trainers and sports socks

- clothing that is unclean

- clothing that is too tight

- too much jewellery

- too much perfume or aftershave.

Be on time.

Look cheerful and smile.

During the interview

- It is important to sell yourself at an interview, while still being truthful.
- Be enthusiastic about yourself and your experiences.
- Give examples of things you have done.
- Answer each question as clearly and precisely as you can.
- Don't slouch in the chair.
- If your mind goes blank, don't panic – ask them to repeat the question.
- Have a few questions prepared, to ask at the end of the interview.

Throughout, remain polite and cheerful, using the interviewer's name if you can.

Questions you could ask during (or straight after) your interview are:

- What are the hours of work?
- Who is the line manager?
- What is a typical client and what are his or her needs?
- How long has the organisation been in existence?

After the interview, you should be told within a few days whether or not you have 'got the job'. Remember – it is not a poor reflection on an individual who does not get a job; it just means that there was another, more experienced or qualified person who applied.

unit 5

Social responsibility at work

In this unit you will begin to think about your working environment. You may be considering employment in a hospital or a residential home, or a job helping people in their homes. All of these working environments are different; however, there are universal rules that apply to all settings in order that the health and safety of you and the people you look after is protected.

You will also look at the ways in which your working practices — what you do at work — can help to protect the environment, and consider why this is important. This means thinking about how you can save money, keep the environment clean and healthy, and maintain good standards of personal hygiene. These things are important not just for you but also for your clients (residents or service users).

In this unit you will learn about:

▷ environmental issues in work

▷ how the law affects people in work.

Energy conservation and recycling

What is social responsibility?

As a member of society, you have a responsibility to other people as well as to yourself. This is what is meant by the term 'social responsibility'.

If you work in the public sector, you are likely to be employed either directly by the government or within organisations that receive government money in order to provide services to the public. You therefore have a responsibility to the public as a whole. This means a responsibility to everybody, whether people are receiving services directly from you or not. Much care work is public sector work, and this responsibility towards the public is known as a 'duty of care'. This principle or idea means that you are responsible for the things that you do (or fail to do) if they have an effect on others.

Social responsibility and the environment

As part of social responsibility, you need to consider the importance of protecting the environment for everyone and particularly for future generations.

● ● ● *Conserving the earth's resources*

It is now recognised that the earth's natural resources, such as oil, trees, fish and minerals, are being used up at a rate that cannot be sustained. Natural fuels such as coal, oil and gas cannot be replaced so it is important to conserve the earth's resources – to use them at a slower rate so they last longer. Each person can make a small contribution to conserving natural resources; the more people who become involved, the more resources can be conserved.

● ● ● *Global warming*

Global warming is causing significant changes in the climate – the temperature and weather patterns – around the world. For example, in the UK, summers have become hotter and drier with an increased risk of drought and winters have become wetter and stormier with an increased risk of flooding: in fact, the 1990s were the warmest decade in the last 100 years. Global warming is a threat to people's health because of the effect that changes in weather patterns will have on food production and the likelihood of increased droughts, flooding and other extremes of weather such as hurricanes. Temperature rises may also bring new diseases against which the population has no natural protection, e.g. malaria.

The main cause of global warming is thought to be 'greenhouse gases' such as:

- carbon dioxide, which is produced when fossil fuels such as wood, coal and oil are burned

- methane, from agriculture and waste management
- CFC gases found in aerosol sprays.

These gases stay in the earth's atmosphere and prevent the heat from the earth being released into space, creating an effect similar to the glass in a greenhouse.

• • • *Environmental pollution*

A landfill site.

Environmental pollution is another problem in modern, consumer societies. For example, factories produce chemical waste, cars give off exhaust fumes, and fertilisers used in farming pollute the land and rivers. Rubbish is another huge source of environmental pollution: 400 million tonnes of waste are produced in England and Wales every year. Most of this rubbish is buried in the ground in landfill sites, and this pollutes the earth for future generations. The government has therefore given local authorities the responsibility for managing waste at a local level and has set targets to reduce the amount of waste currently buried in landfill sites.

Recycling

The door to door collection of materials for recycling.

You can effectively minimise the amount of new materials you use by recycling. Recycling means re-using something, and it helps to conserve materials and scarce resources.

In the past, recycling was quite common. For example, milk was delivered to your door by the milkman in glass bottles, which were then returned to be cleaned and used again. Soft drinks, cordial and beer also came in glass bottles; when the bottles were empty, if you took them back to the shop you were given a small amount of money (a useful source of spending money for many children!).

Today, many drinks are sold in plastic bottles that are simply thrown away. It is estimated that recycling just one plastic bottle would save enough energy to power a 60-watt light bulb for six hours. However, only 3 per cent of household bottles are currently recycled. Plastic does not break down over time (it is not bio-degradable) so it remains in landfill sites for a very long time. (Examples of bio-degradable containers include waxed and treated cardboard or paper.)

Materials that can be recycled include paper, glass, aluminium and steel cans, textiles, plastics, organic waste, furniture, batteries, and electrical and electronic equipment. There are many ingenious ways of recycling broken items and waste products into useful items, e.g. you can recycle plastic bottles by refilling them or using them for something else. However, it is important to remember that some products and equipment used in the health, social care and early years sectors cannot be re-used because this might cause cross-infection of germs and bacteria.

Some common recycling labels.

◖◖◖ EVIDENCE ACTIVITY

Recycling

1 Find out what your local council is doing to help conservation and recycling, and what facilities are available in your local area. You can find information about recycling in your local area in your library or on the Internet (enter your council's name into a search engine). Find out if there are any facilities for collecting:

▢ glass   ▢ paper   ▢ plastic   ▢ cans.

2 Are the recycling facilities nearby and easily accessible?

3 Does your council provide a doorstep–collection recycling service?

4 Make a list of the things you use at work everyday that could be collected for recycling.

● ● ● *Recycling office products and equipment*

Office products and equipment can be recycled as follows:

- shredded paper can be composted
- toner and ink cartridges from printers can be refilled
- paper and envelopes can be recycled
- some computers and office equipment can be recycled.

Many local authorities have contracts with organisations specialising in recycling. Detailed information about what can be recycled and where can be found on the following websites:

- www.crn.org.uk – Community Recycling Network;
- www.wrap.org.uk – Waste and Resources Action Programme;
- www.letsrecycle.com – news and information about recycling and waste management.

GIVE IT A GO recycling labels

Next time you are in the supermarket, examine how different products are packaged. Look for labels that show if the container can be recycled (see opposite).

These labels are found on different types of plastic and on other materials. The arrows indicate that the item can be recycled.

Each type of plastic has a standard marking code (number and letters) to help identify the type of plastic to make sorting and recycling easier. For example, PVC stands for *polyvinyl chloride* and is used mainly for food trays, cling film and plastic bottles for things such as shampoo. LDPE stands for *low density polyethylene*, used for carrier bags and bin liners. HDPE is *high density polyethylene* which is stronger and used for items such as milk bottles and washing-up liquid. These are just a few examples; there are about fifty different groups of plastic, each with many variations.

1 Find four items that are in containers that can be recycled.

2 Find four items that are made from recycled material.

3 Find four items that are double wrapped (unnecessary packaging).

● ● ● *Recycling organic waste*

Other things that can be recycled include leftover uncooked vegetables, fruit and plants from the garden, otherwise known as organic waste. Vegetable peelings, eggshells and tea leaves or teabags can be made into compost for gardens. Compost is produced when these organic substances start to break down and decay. This is a natural process that happens, for example, when dead leaves and twigs decay back into the soil. Compost nourishes the soil and helps new plants to grow.

CASE STUDY environmental changes

Consider this case study and think about the changes you could make to either your work environment or your home.

Angela works in a residential home for fifteen residents situated in open countryside. Angela has noticed that there is always lots of rubbish in the kitchen bin when the cook leaves each afternoon. She discusses with the manager about starting to make compost from the waste, to use in the garden of the home.

CASE STUDY) environmental changes continued

Angela goes to the library for a gardening book and finds out that the Local Authority will provide free composting bins if you also purchase a water butt. The manager agrees that Angela can go ahead with the purchase because a water butt collects rainwater to use in the garden. Before she does this, Angela talks to Mrs Greaves, the cook, about composting the kitchen waste. Mrs Greaves points out that they cannot compost leftover cooked food or meat as there are rules against this at present. They make a list of all the things they could put into the composting bin and put a notice on the wall.

It is agreed that the residents should be involved in the project and a meeting is held. It turns out that Tom and Annie, two of the residents, used to be keen gardeners and would like to be involved with the project to re-design the garden so that there are features all the residents can enjoy, such as a vegetable and herb section, and a sensory area with a water feature and scented flowers.

The project is a huge success and six months later the residents are enjoying tea in the garden with lettuce and tomatoes they have grown themselves.

Energy conservation

You can help the environment by using less energy, which also has the advantage of saving money. Most energy is used for heating, lighting, cooking and powering electrical goods.

Within the care sector, particularly in care homes for older people, it is important to keep a balance between conserving energy and ensuring health and safety. However, the following energy conservation ideas are worth considering.

• • • *Low-energy lightbulbs*

Low-energy lightbulbs cost more to purchase (around £5) than ordinary lightbulbs, but they generally last for about three years, which is ten to twelve times longer than ordinary lightbulbs. Each lightbulb is estimated to save £7 per year on the electricity bill.

■■■ EVIDENCE ACTIVITY

Low-energy lightbulbs

1 Walk around your workplace and count the number of lightbulbs. If you are not currently working, you can do this activity for your own home.

2 Work out how much money could be saved in electricity bills if they were all replaced with low-energy lightbulbs. (Don't forget to deduct the cost of buying the bulbs from the amount likely to be saved.)

3 Work out a plan for gradually replacing them with low-energy lightbulbs.

For more ideas and examples see:

▷ www.saveenergy.co.uk

▷ www.actionenergy.org.uk — a care homes fact sheet is available as well as details of contacts that can visit your home or organisation and advise on ways of saving energy.

● ● ● *Turning down the heating*

If the central heating is turned down by 1 or 2 degrees Celsius, this will save energy. While it is important for older people to stay warm, they can be encouraged to do more movement and exercise. This has the double advantage of helping older people to keep warm and remain active and mobile. It is useful to have a temperature control such as a thermostat in each room so that, for example, one room could be kept warmer for residents who felt cold or were unable to exercise. Residents would benefit from some activity everyday and could be consulted about their preferences, e.g. movement and exercise classes, gentle yoga stretches and breathing exercises, accompanied short walks or movement to music. The same principles would apply if you were helping someone in their own home.

● ● ● *Washing machines and dishwashers*

To save energy, ensure that washing machines and dishwashers are always full when operating. If not, many washing machines have a half-load programme. Some machines have special features for using less water and detergent, and many are labelled with a code that indicates how energy efficient they are compared with similar models.

When using washing machines for heavily soiled or contaminated articles, you should rinse them off first and use a pre-wash programme. You can then wash the articles at a lower temperature. This is more energy efficient than using a high temperature for a full-wash programme. The same principle applies when using a dishwasher: use a rinse programme to remove debris from the plates then wash on a less intensive programme when full. You can also rinse dishes by hand before loading them into the dishwasher, which will use less water.

● ● ● *Electrical goods*

Articles such as kettles, toasters and irons often have energy saving features. For example, kettles that switch off once the water has boiled and irons that go on to standby if not used for a given period. These are also safety features that could prevent fires if the items were left on accidentally.

Televisions and other electrical equipment that can be left on standby should be turned off whenever possible (sometimes this interferes with programming features) because it is estimated that a television on standby uses almost as much electricity as when it is on. It is also a fire hazard.

It is more efficient to fill a kettle with just enough water for your needs than to boil a full kettle for one cup of tea. It is not good to keep boiling the same water in any case, as it evaporates and any minerals in the water become more concentrated.

● ● ● *Hot water*

It is important that hot water is stored at a temperature that is high enough to prevent the bacteria that causes Legionnaire's Disease from multiplying. (Legionnaire's Disease is an infection of the lungs, similar to pneumonia and caused by bacteria.) This is a recommended temperature of 60 degrees Celsius by the National Minimum Standards for Older People, which is part of the regulatory framework for this group of clients. To achieve 60 degrees Celsius as efficiently and cost-effectively as possible, a hot water thermostat (temperature control) should be fitted to the hot water system. Hot water storage cylinders also need to have a thick insulating jacket (lagging) to keep the water hot for longer, since the thermostat reheats the water when it drops below the set temperature.

However, water at a temperature of 60 degrees Celsius is hot enough to cause scalding on sensitive skin. An ideal water temperature for tap use is around 43 degrees Celsius. To achieve this, a valve can be fitted to the tap supply to cool the water that comes from the hot water tank.

Finally, you need to make sure that you always put the plug in the sink so that hot water is not wasted.

A cleaner environment

● ● ● *Air quality*

Air pollution levels vary depending on the area where you live. Pollution is directly related to the amount and type of industry in your local area and the volume of traffic. It has been estimated that if each person took one less car journey a week – an average distance of nine miles – traffic pollution could be cut by 13 per cent. The Environment Agency, set up by the government to monitor pollution and improve the environment, names the worst areas for pollution on its website (www.environment-agency.gov.uk).

The weather also has an effect on air quality. Next time the weather is warm, sunny and calm, look around. You will probably see the distant horizon in a haze, especially in towns and cities. This is atmospheric pollution. It has a significant effect on health, particularly for older people and young children, and for people with breathing conditions like asthma. If there is no wind then atmospheric pollution is not blown away but stays low and is inhaled. The main atmospheric pollutants are listed below.

Name of pollutant	Effect of pollutant on human health
Sulphur Dioxide (SO_2)	Coughing, tightening of chest, irritation of lungs.
Nitrogen Dioxide (NO_2)	Irritation and inflammation of lungs.
Particulate Matter	Inflammation of lungs, worsening of symptoms for people with heart and lung conditions, links with coronary heart disease and lung cancer.
Carbon Monoxide (CO)	Prevents normal movement of oxygen in the blood causing reduced oxygen supply to the heart.
Ozone	Pain on deep breathing, coughing, irritation and inflammation of lungs.
Benzene	A cause of cancer.
Lead	Linked to impaired mental function and lower intelligence (IQ) in children.

● ● ● *Air quality in the home*

Internal air quality will vary according to:

- whether smoking is allowed in shared areas
- the time of year and opportunities for ventilation
- the general cleanliness of the environment, including the amount of dust in the air.

Some people believe that smoking should be banned in public places such as restaurants and pubs. They argue that everybody has a right to clean air and that smoking is a health hazard. What do you think?

● ● ● *Alternative methods of transport*

There is no doubt that cars are one of the biggest causes of pollution and environmental damage:

- Exhaust fumes from traffic pollute the air.
- More and more roads need to be built to keep pace with the increase in car ownership, destroying countryside and wildlife habitats.
- Cars kill people regularly on our roads, although the UK has one of the best records for road safety in Europe.

- Cars need maintaining – they use up resources such as oil and petrol (fossil fuels which are non-renewable), rubber for tyres, huge amounts of plastic (made with oil from fossil fuels) and metal.
- Dirty and used oil, old tyres and asbestos brake linings all have to be disposed of safely because they are health hazards.
- Cars that have reached the end of their useful life are scrapped, contributing to waste.

Many environmental specialists think that cars are an extravagance the planet cannot afford and that we need to use other methods of transport. Different local authorities have different transport policies to discourage excessive car use, for example, cycle lanes and traffic calming schemes such as road narrowing in residential areas. Some local authorities provide subsidised public transport for different groups of people, such as the elderly, children and people on low incomes.

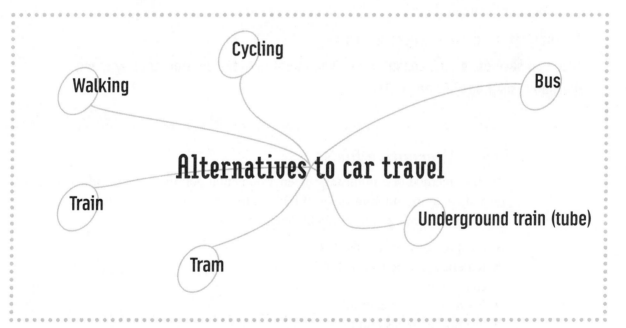

Unfortunately, people often have negative attitudes about public transport. This is because public transport can be crowded during the rush hour and run late. Some people think that if you use public transport it is because you can't afford to own and run a car. Cars are associated with wealth and status, a view that is encouraged by adverts.

As a worker in the health, social care and early years sectors, you need to be aware of the transport policies in your local area, including what your local council is doing to help reduce car use. For example, if there are cheap fares available on public transport, this information could be shared with others in your setting.

◼◼◼ EVIDENCE ACTIVITY

Travelling to work

1 Talk to colleagues about how they get to work or what their usual method of transport is. Ask them why this is their preferred means of transport.

2 Consider how you might make changes that would benefit the environment. These might include car sharing, cycling or walking.

3 Find out what problems there are with using public transport for work, for example, shift patterns or unsocial hours.

4 When you have considered the alternatives, rank them with your colleagues, taking into account the benefits to the environment, the cost and the health benefits.

▷ Which method is the most environmentally friendly?

▷ Which is the cheapest?

▷ Which is the most practical and why?

Once you have done this, consider how you might help the environment by using alternative methods of transport.

••• Alternative fuels

Another method of minimising the environmental pollution from traffic is to develop and use different types of fuels. Alternative cleaner fuels that are gradually becoming more available include:

- compressed natural gas (CNG)
- liquefied petroleum gas (LPG)
- city diesel
- hydrogen (not common)
- alcohol fuels (also unusual)
- battery-operated vehicles.

It remains to be seen whether this technology will produce transport that protects rather than pollutes the environment.

Public health and the workplace

Public health refers to everybody's health. As a worker in the health, social care and early years sectors, the health of the public should be your concern. It is important that you behave in a responsible and professional manner towards clients and service users, and set a good example. You need to be aware of the

health messages that the government gives to the public and promote these messages, irrespective of your own personal beliefs. This is because you become a 'public servant' when you work in the health, social care and early years sectors, since the government pays you either directly or indirectly through your employer (who receives government funding to provide a service to the public).

Waste disposal

Within the health, social care and early years sectors, there are two main aspects to waste disposal:

1 Non-clinical waste

This includes packaging, paper and general rubbish. It can be disposed of through the normal refuse collection procedures for domestic and business waste.

2 Clinical waste

This includes contaminated (used) material, for example, dressings, needles, catheters and soiled protective items such as disposable pads. Many of these items are contaminated with body fluids. There are special measures for disposing of this waste. It has to be placed in special bags and collected by an organisation licensed to dispose of it. (Information about the disposal of clinical waste can be found on www.defra.gov.uk.)

● ● ● *The health hazards of waste*

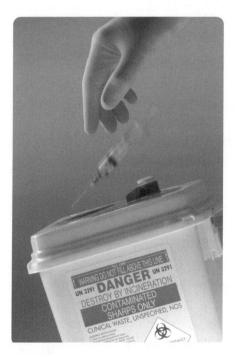

A container for disposing of clinical waste.

While ordinary waste and rubbish is dirty and unpleasant, it only becomes a health hazard if it is not disposed of quickly and efficiently. The main problems arise from rotting waste matter, which smells bad, contains high levels of bacteria and attracts flies and, in extreme cases, vermin such as rats and mice. These effects are more likely in warm weather because waste rots more quickly when warm. This is because the bacteria in the waste are able to multiply more quickly.

Clinical waste is a direct hazard to health because it is contaminated, either through contact with infectious material or with bodily fluids that are potentially infectious. Needle injuries, cuts and abrasions from clinical waste can lead to infection. The staff member involved usually needs to have time off work and he or she may need counselling, both of which are expensive for the organisation. If the person becomes infected or suffers illness as a direct result of the setting's policies and procedures not being followed, he or she can sue those responsible for health and safety at work. The organisation may be fined and the individual awarded financial compensation.

Policies on smoking and alcohol

• • • *Smoking policies at work*

Many workplaces now have policies that mean smoking and alcohol are prohibited (not allowed) on the premises in the interests of public health. Many public places such as restaurants and cinemas have smoking bans or allow smoking only in certain areas. It is particularly important that the health, social care and early years sectors are seen to promote healthy living practices such as non-smoking. However, in some settings a ban on smoking and alcohol can give rise to conflict and confusion unless clear policies and procedures are established.

Anti-smoking policies are very sensible in places like hospitals, where people are usually acutely ill and on medication. However, in residential homes it is important that the residents feel at home. This means that they should be free to behave as they would in their own homes, which may include smoking and drinking if these are normal habits for them. However, this can be unacceptable to other residents and unhealthy for them.

WHAT if

Work policies

... *You were the manager of a residential home?*

1 Should staff who work in a residential home be encouraged to give up smoking in order to set an example to others and for the sake of their health?

2 Do staff have a right to smoke during their break even if they are still on work premises?

3 Should residents be allowed to smoke in their bedrooms?

4 What about residents and staff who don't smoke? What are their rights?

Find out what the policy on smoking is in your workplace. If possible, find out from local residential homes how they manage these conflicting issues.

• • • *Policies on alcohol*

Alcohol consumption is a regular aspect of social life for many people. While moderate drinking is not harmful for young people, it may cause health problems in older people. This is because the body becomes less tolerant to alcohol as you get older. Alcohol can also be dangerous if taken with medicines, particularly tranquillisers, sedatives, sleeping pills and painkillers. Some cold remedies can also be dangerous if taken with alcohol.

CASE STUDY   alcohol policy

Mary is a domiciliary care worker. She regularly visits Mrs Mason to assist her with washing and dressing. Mrs Mason has developed a chronic chest condition that leaves her short of breath after the slightest effort; she has been a heavy smoker all her life. Mary has become concerned about Mrs Mason's health. She often seems very tired and confused in the morning, and is unsteady on her feet. Mrs Mason says it is because of the sleeping pills that the doctor has given her.

One day, as Mary is tidying the kitchen, she finds a half-empty bottle of whisky in a cupboard that is not used often. She is worried that Mrs Mason has been drinking and that this is why her health seems to be deteriorating.

1 Should Mary:

(a) confront Mrs Mason and ask her if she has been drinking

(b) tell Mrs Mason's relatives

(c) tell Mrs Mason's GP

(d) report back to the care agency who employs her?

Give reasons for your answer.

2 Find out what facilities there are in your area to support older drinkers and what the alcohol policy is in your local residential care home. Can residents have a glass of wine with meals? Is alcohol allowed only on special occasions?

Personal hygiene

It is important to keep a good standard of personal hygiene as a care worker because people who are ill or frail generally have less resistance to disease. Good standards of personal hygiene help to prevent cross-infection.

It is also highly unpleasant to be in close contact with someone who has body odour or smells of stale cigarettes and last night's alcohol! You should always take care to wash regularly and wear a clean uniform.

• • • *Personal appearance*

You may find in your setting that there are rules about what you can and cannot wear for work. There is also likely to be some kind of uniform and you may also be asked to wear thin latex gloves when helping clients. This is important in order to prevent cross-infection, whether germs are passed from yourself to another person or from that person to you.

Jewellery, apart from wedding rings and stud earrings, is best avoided because it is a possible source of cross-infection. In addition, while you are working you may catch it against something or someone, damaging the jewellery and hurting yourself or them. Similarly, you could quite easily damage the skin of a frail or sick person with your jewellery while moving or handling him or her.

• • • Hand washing

Germs and bacteria are normally found on your skin – particularly on the hands, under the nails, and in skin folds and creases. This means that if you do not regularly wash your hands, infection can easily spread from one person to another. Regular hand washing and the provision of adequate facilities for this, e.g. soap and paper tissues for drying hands, is therefore very important in the care setting.

Remember: the most effective way of preventing cross-infection is by washing your hands!

Most people do not wash their hands properly – including healthcare workers. Since the hands are covered with microbes (germs), which are on everything we touch, hand washing is the single most effective method of infection control. Artificial nails and chipped nail varnish are health hazards because they increase the areas where germs could hide and prevent you from seeing any dirt under your nails. Also, wearing gloves does not mean that your hands do not need to be washed regularly.

• • • When to wash your hands

You should *always* wash your hands:

- After direct contact with individual patients, residents or clients and before dealing with the next person.
- Before performing any clinical activity with clients, such as dealing with catheters or dressings (invasive procedures).
- Before preparing, handling, serving or eating food, and before feeding a patient.
- When your hands are visibly dirty.
- If your hands are likely to have come into contact with blood, faeces, pus or other bodily fluids, even if you have been wearing gloves.
- After removing your gloves.
- After personal body functions, such as using the toilet or blowing your nose.
- Whenever you are in doubt about the need to do so – if in doubt, WASH.

Don't forget that patients, clients and residents should be helped to wash their hands before meals, after going to the bathroom and before leaving their room.

• • • How to wash your hands effectively

1   Remove any jewellery before washing your hands so that all areas of the skin can be washed.

2 Rinse your hands under warm running water to wash away loose bacteria and germs.

3 Lather with soap, rubbing your hands together; use about a teaspoonful of liquid soap.

4 Cover all surfaces of the hands and fingers for at least 10 seconds, and longer if your hands are visibly dirty. Frequently missed areas are: the thumbs, under the nails, and the backs of the fingers and hands.

5 Rinse your hands under warm running water to wash off any remaining soap and loosened bacteria and germs.

6 Dry your hands thoroughly with a disposable paper towel or an air dryer; this will reduce the number of germs remaining on the hands. Germs can remain on cloth towels and re-contaminate hands.

7 Turn off the tap without touching it with the hands, if possible, to avoid re-contaminating the hands. It is best if taps on sinks used for hand washing have a lever action that can be operated with elbows or wrists.

8 It is important to keep hands in good condition. Protective and moisturising hand lotion should be available to staff, preferably in a wall-mounted pump dispenser.

It is best if taps for hand washing have a lever action that can be operated with elbows or wrists.

There is no evidence that washing with anti-bacterial soap is any more effective than plain soap. However, there may be some advantages when there is an infection present or heavy soiling, e.g. by faeces. It is best to use liquid soap in a wall-mounted dispenser or small, frequently changed bars of soap.

Health at work

You will be expected to be in good general health to work in the health, social care and early years sectors. You should be up-to-date with all relevant immunisations because you will come into contact with many infectious agents and it is important that your body can resist disease. In other words, you need a healthy immune system.

When you first begin health, social care and early years work, you may find that you suffer from more minor ailments such as colds or stomach bugs during the first few months. This is quite normal; it is due to being in close contact with other infections. Eventually, however, this will strengthen your immune system and you will be less likely to become ill.

• • • *Health checks*

Many large organisations, such as NHS Trusts, have an occupational health department that checks the health of employees regularly. Employees may be offered, for example, immunisations against Hepatitis B or screening checks for diseases they may have been in contact with such as tuberculosis. Other organisations buy-in these services on behalf of their staff. Some organisations employ an occupational health nurse who has received special training in industrial diseases, first aid and preventative health.

• • • *Health insurance*

Private healthcare schemes and policies for employees are offered by some companies. These are similar to insurance policies: you pay a fixed amount each month so that, if you become ill, the treatment has already been paid for. There will always be funds to pay for treatment on the condition that enough people pay into the scheme. This is because not everyone will require medical treatment at the same time.

Private health insurance is very good for occasional or emergency treatment. However, if you have a chronic health problem, you may not be allowed to join the scheme. This is because you may require more treatment than the average person and use up more than your share of the costs.

You will probably have a medical examination before you are allowed to join a healthcare scheme. If you are thought to take risks with your health, for example, if you are a smoker, you may not be allowed to join the scheme or you may have to pay more than others do. Your employer may also be prepared to pay into the scheme on your behalf since it will help you to remain healthy and should result in your needing less time off work with sickness. However, if you leave your job, your employer's contributions will stop and you will have to pay your own contributions if you want to remain insured.

The law and work

Laws exist so that people can live together safely and harmoniously. They are designed to protect individuals from both physical and emotional harm, and to punish those who would harm others. The law applies to both property and people, covering all areas of life. Laws are, in fact, rules for living.

As a worker in the health, social care and early years sectors, there are two main groups of laws that are important to you:

1 Laws that protect you in your employment and at work.

2 Laws that protect the people that you care for.

Laws are made by the government through Acts of Parliament and are also known as 'legislation'. Laws that govern working arrangements between employers and employees are called employment laws, for example, the Employment Rights Act 1996. Other legislation covers safety in the workplace, for example, the Health and Safety at Work Act 1974. Both of these types of law are designed to protect you at work. The title of the legislation shows the year in which the law came into force. Sometimes laws are modified and updated; the title of the law will show that the Act has been amended.

Different organisations have been set up by the government to monitor and apply the law on its behalf. One example is the Health and Safety Executive, who are responsible for investigating accidents at work to see if an employer has broken health and safety laws.

Employers can be fined or, in serious cases, sent to prison if they are found guilty of breaking the law, especially if this has resulted in an injury to someone. This is true even if the person was not an employee because the employer is responsible for the health and safety of everyone on the premises. When large organisations are found to be in breach of (have broken) health and safety regulations, the senior executives and chief members of the organisation's management can be held jointly responsible. This is called 'corporate responsibility'.

Employment law

Under employment law, both employers and employees have rights and responsibilities towards each other.

• • • *Employee rights*

- Employees must have a contract of employment that gives details of their hours of work, pay and holiday entitlements (Employment Rights Act 1996).
- Employees are entitled to a written statement of the key terms and conditions of their employment within two months of starting work, providing the work contract is for longer than one month.
- Employees have a right to be treated equally with others doing the same or similar jobs and they are entitled to a minimum wage. This means that it is illegal to pay someone less than the minimum wage; employers can be taken to court if they do.
- Employees can be sacked only in certain circumstances. If an employee feels that they have been unfairly treated, they can take their claim to an industrial tribunal. The tribunal is similar to a court and will make a judgment about who is right.
- Employees must be given time off for certain activities such as jury service or trade union activities.
- Harassment and bullying at work is an offence and employers can be held

responsible for failing to act if such incidents have been reported to them through the proper procedures and no steps have subsequently been taken.

The law protects *all* workers, including pregnant women and part-time employees.

• • • *Employer rights*

- Employers have a right to ensure that the person they are intending to employ is a fit person for the job. This is very important in the health, social care and early years sectors. Employers must be able to check the employee's past record via the Criminal Records Bureau, to see if he or she is fit to work with vulnerable people.
- Your employer is entitled to hold personal information about you such as your address; however, personal information cannot be shared without your permission because it is protected under the Data Protection Act 1998.

Each organisation has procedures that employees need to know about to ensure that they fulfill their responsibilities as an employee.

CASE STUDY) employment law

Seema has been working part-time as a care assistant for three years at Cherry Trees Residential Home. She has recently discovered that she is pregnant and is worried about the heavy work she often has to do, especially when the home is short of staff due to sickness and absence.

1 What are Seema's entitlements under Employment Law?

2 What action does she need to take?

• • • *Health and Safety at Work Act 1974*

This Act has been designed to protect employee's safety at work. It covers areas such as the use of equipment, heating and lighting requirements, meal breaks and the length of time you are permitted to work without a break. For example, employers must ensure that the workplace has:

- adequate ventilation – stale air which is warm and humid should be diluted with clean fresh air drawn from outside, and air should be circulated without causing draughts
- a temperature of between 13 and 16 degrees Celsius, depending on how much physical effort the work requires; special measures such as extra breaks and protective clothing need to be provided for workers in very hot or cold workplaces (e.g. foundries or frozen food factories)

- lighting that allows people to work safely: local light sources may need to be provided in some cases, e.g. at nurse workstations on a ward at night; emergency lighting must be provided where a sudden blackout would be dangerous
- facilities for workers to take regular breaks, usually every four hours.

The Act also requires that employers undertake an assessment of the risks in the workplace to employees and others, and establish systems and policies to safeguard their health, safety and welfare. The Act applies to equipment and methods of work and covers activities, machinery and substances.

In health, social care and early years work, health and safety regulations cover moving and handling. This includes handling hazardous substances, which is covered by COSHH regulations (Care of Substances Hazardous to Health). Employees have a responsibility to know, understand and follow those procedures that have been put in place to protect them; for example, wearing protective clothing and completing the correct paperwork if an incident occurs.

Other important working laws

Many laws about work are concerned with the fair treatment of all people. As such, they affect how you are treated at work and are often referred to as 'equal opportunities legislation'. The main legislation includes:

● ● ● *Equal Pay Act 1970*

This Act made it illegal to pay women less than men for doing the same job or one requiring the same level of skill, qualifications and responsibility. Despite this, women's average earnings still do not equal those of men. For example, the national average earnings for a man in full-time employment is currently £27,300 per year; for women, it is £20,592 per year. The Equal Opportunities Commission suggests there are three main reasons for this:

1 Discrimination in pay systems: women are being paid less then men for the same job despite this being illegal. Many women do not know how much their male colleagues earn because it is not considered polite to ask.

2 Occupational segregation: the majority of women work in specific occupations that are traditionally low-paid, such as catering, cleaning and caring.

3 Caring responsibilities: the responsibility for looking after children and other relatives still falls mainly on women. This affects their promotion at work and career progression.

● ● ● *National Minimum Wage 1998*

This Act introduced a national minimum wage for the first time in the UK. This means that it is illegal to pay anybody less than the national minimum wage.

The national minimum wage is currently:

- £4.50 per hour for people over 22 years of age;
- £3.80 for people aged between 18 and 21 years and for some employees on specific types of training scheme.

The Low Pay Commission monitors this Act and provides advice for those who are having difficulties with an employer.

• • • Sex Discrimination Act 1975

This Act made it illegal to discriminate (provide less favourable services, goods or facilities) to people because of their sex (gender). The Act covers many areas of life including employment, pay, housing, education, and goods and services. Some employment is exempt (does not need to comply with the Act) for specific reasons. For example, it might not be appropriate or helpful for men to be employed as counsellors for women survivors of rape or sexual assault.

• • • Race Relations Act 1976

This is another law concerned with the fair treatment of people from different races or ethnic backgrounds. It makes discrimination on the basis of skin colour or ethnicity illegal. Despite this, some individuals continue to receive less than favourable treatment as a result of their race or ethnic background. Such discrimination has been highlighted recently in cases where whole organisations, including those concerned with health and social care, have been accused of having a discriminatory culture.

• • • Disability Discrimination Act 1995

This Act is aimed at the fair treatment of disabled people. It requires that organisations ensure that their premises and services are accessible to disabled people. It aims to ensure that disabled people have the same opportunity of access to activities, facilities, goods and services as anyone else. It also covers employment and buying or renting land or property.

• • • Data Protection Act 1998

This law was established to protect people's rights when organisations hold information about them. It covers both paper and electronic information. Organisations that hold personal information about individuals have legal obligations to ensure that the information is used fairly and lawfully, and only for limited purposes, in a way that does not breach the individual's rights. However, some organisations have been accused of using this law as an excuse for not sharing information that could have helped people receive better services or protection from harm. The NHS has therefore produced a Code of Practice on confidentiality, to help carers understand their responsibilities towards the people they care for.

• • • *Human Rights Act 1998*

This law is based on the European Convention of Human Rights, which is now part of UK law. This Act protects some basic human rights and freedoms, such as:

- the right to life
- the right not to be subjected to degrading or inhuman treatment
- the right to marry and enjoy family life
- the right to a fair trial
- the right to freedom of expression, association and assembly (this means the freedom to express your views, whatever they are; the freedom to join clubs or groups, including political groups and trades unions; the freedom to gather together in groups with like-minded people).

If individuals feel that their rights have been ignored (breached), they can challenge public authority and public bodies (organisations) under this law.

Laws that protect people who receive care services

The laws described on pages 151–153 apply to everyone, including those people receiving care. It is therefore important that you know what your responsibilities for protecting other people are, as well as how the law protects you. There are, however, particular laws that are concerned with the delivery of care services and the protection of those receiving care; these are outlined below.

• • • *The Care Standards Act 2000*

This legislation states the standards of care that should be provided to different groups of people who receive a range of different care services. The Act includes information on how the health, social care and early years sectors should be regulated. In particular, it covers:

- the registration and regulation of practitioners (individuals delivering care)
- the registration and regulation of organisations that provide care services.

The Act also states the National Minimum Standards of Care. This covers things such as the level of training that staff should have for particular roles, the type of accommodation that should be provided for different groups and, in some cases, the minimum number of staff. Inspections take place to ensure that these regulations are being followed and vary according to the type of service being provided. For example, residential care homes and children's homes will be inspected twice per year; however, independent healthcare establishments and agencies, fostering and adoption agencies and residential special schools will only be inspected annually. Other types of services such as boarding schools will be inspected once every three years, since they will also be subjected to education inspections by Ofsted (Office for Standards in Education).

● ● ● *The Children Act 1989*

The Children Act 1989 and its amendments cover:

- the rights of children to be protected, especially from abuse
- the duties of parents and carers
- the rights of children to be consulted about arrangements for their care.

Other acts are designed to protect different groups, for example, The Mental Health Act 1983, which is concerned with the admission of people to psychiatric hospitals for their own safety or the safety of others. Individuals can be admitted to hospital against their will if doctors and social workers feel that they need treatment. A new Act of Parliament (called a Bill until it is officially passed) was drafted in 2002 to amend the 1983 Act, but it has not yet been agreed. Different rules apply in Scotland, where a new Act – Mental Health (Care and Treatment) – was passed in 2003. More information can be found on mental health at the website for the National Institute for Mental Health in England (part of the NHS Modernisation Agency), www.nimhe.org.uk.

◉◉◉ EVIDENCE ACTIVITY

Laws and work

1 Identify the key points of four Acts of Parliament (laws) that are concerned with either

   (a) your area of work

   (b) the area of work that you are most interested in.

   The Acts can be about either your client group or about working arrangements or practices.

2 Make a poster that gives details of one of the four Acts you have chosen. Your poster should identify:

   ▢ the key points of the Act

   ▢ how it helps or protects client or workers

   ▢ who (what organisation or regulatory body) is responsible for ensuring the Act is obeyed

   ▢ what penalties are likely if the law is broken.

unit 6

Health and the environment

In this unit you will look at how the environment in which we live and work can affect our health, safety and well-being. You will learn to recognise the sorts of things that can become a risk to our health or the health of others in the community, and examine the ways in which these risks can be minimised. You will also begin to think about how people can work together and organise themselves to raise awareness of issues that affect their health and well-being. Finally, we will look at what you can do to improve your environment.

In this unit you will learn about:

▷ the different environmental hazards that can affect people and communities

▷ how to carry out an investigation of an environmental issue

▷ how to raise awareness of environmental issues that affect people and communities.

Types of environment

Human beings are very adaptable: they can, and do, live in a whole variety of environments, from the South American rainforests to the frozen Alaskan steppes. In this unit you will examine your local environment – your surroundings, or the area where you live or work. You will consider the hazards that you regularly come across in your environment and how these affect both your health and well-being and that of people in your local community.

External environments

The environment includes surroundings that are both visible and invisible, for example, the physical surroundings that you see and the air that you breathe. It contains all the things that you need for survival so it can affect your health in many ways. For example, it is estimated that around 80 per cent of cancers have an environmental cause. The environment affects not just your physical health but also your psychological health and well-being (state of mind). This is because your environment can affect how you feel, and this affects your mood. In a safe and pleasant environment, you are much less likely to feel depressed and sad.

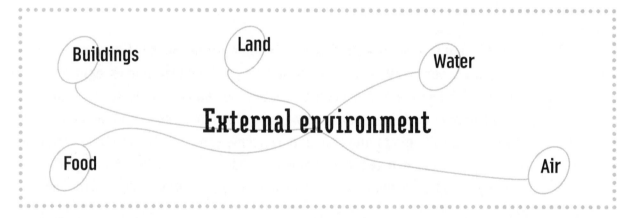

The health, safety and well-being of the population are the responsibility of the government, and this includes responsibility for the environment. To minimise the risks to health from the external environment, the government has made laws concerning:

- land use
- air quality
- water quality
- waste disposal.

• • • *Macro environments*

'Macro' is a term used to describe things that are large. Macro environments can be described as large public spaces. They include things like your geographical location – where you live, including the part of the country that you live in, whether you live in a city, town or village, and whether you live in a part of the country that is very flat, very hilly or near the sea. The place where you live will affect your lifestyle, such as your opportunities for work and leisure. Today, most people in the UK live in towns and cities. Macro environments also include the sort of industry you might find in a particular area, such as manufacturing or agriculture, and the public facilities available, such as parks and open spaces.

GIVE IT A GO   macro environments

Visit your local library and examine different maps of the UK. Try and identify which parts of the country are hilly and which are flat. Identify the different counties if you can, e.g. Wiltshire, Cornwall and Lancashire. Which areas of the country have most towns? Which have least? How many large cities are there? (You can also get this information from the Internet.)

• • • *Describing different external environments*

There are different ways to describe different types of external environment. For example:

- An 'urban' or 'built' environment usually refers to a town or city and includes both housing and office or commercial space.
- Areas of residential housing on the edge of a large town or city are called 'suburbs'. These are often close to open countryside but with good transport links to the city or town centre.
- A 'rural' or 'green' environment usually means the countryside and includes both farms and small towns or villages.
- 'Industrial' environments are those with factories or work units, such as an industrial estate. Many towns grew up around a main industry, particularly in the North and Midlands, with houses built near to the factories. More recently,

An industrial environment in the north of England.

industry is found on the outskirts of towns and close to transport links, e.g. motorway networks.

- The 'natural' environment is a term that is often used to describe geographical areas where few people live, such as mountainous regions, deserts or jungle. These areas have not been affected by human activity such as farming or agriculture.

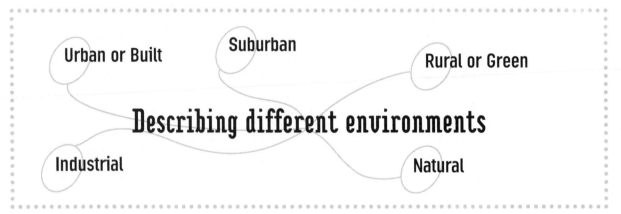

Urban or Built
Suburban
Rural or Green

Describing different environments

Industrial
Natural

CASE STUDY describing environments

Read the descriptions below and see if you can identify the type of environment that each person lives in.

Lee Chiang:

Lee is 9 years old. He lives with his mother, father, older brother and younger sister in a semi-detached house situated on a leafy avenue on the outskirts of the city. There are many similar houses nearby. Lee's house has a garden, central heating and a garage, since the family owns two cars. His father travels into the city every day to his work at a bank.

Robert Greenwood:

Robert lives with his mother and two sisters in a terraced house with two bedrooms. The house is heated with gas fires and there is no garden or garage, although there is a backyard. The house is situated in a street of similar houses close to the town centre. Robert is at college studying to be an electrician. His mother works part-time at the local factory making biscuits.

Laura Price:

Laura has lived in the same house all her life because it used to belong to her grandparents. It is a large farmhouse beneath a steep hill, where the family graze sheep. The house is at the end of a long track, five miles from the village. The house is surrounded by several outbuildings and has a vegetable garden.

CASE STUDY describing environments continued

Wesley Smith:
Wesley is 10 years old and lives in a two-bedroom flat on the fourth floor of a high-rise block of flats. There are three more blocks of flats nearby. Wesley lives with his mother and father, older sister and baby brother. The flat is heated by electric central heating. There is no garden, although there is a playground across the road. Wesley's father works as a bus driver.

▷ What sort of environment do you live in?

• • • *Local industry*

Wherever you live, there will be some kind of local industry. This may be:

- agriculture or farming, which involves growing crops for human and animal consumption or rearing animals for wool and dairy products
- manufacturing of goods, such as cars or household equipment
- office-based, for example, financial services, which includes insurance and banking.

It is important that you know what types of industry are in your local area because they all have different effects on health. For example, manufacturing and 'heavy industry', which involves turning raw materials such as metal into goods, is likely to be more polluting to the atmosphere than office-based industry. However, the health of office-based workers may be affected by office equipment such as computers or photocopiers.

GIVE IT A GO industry and health

1 Using the Internet, find out which industries present the most danger to health from:

   ▷ accidents

   ▷ injuries

   ▷ hazardous substances.

2 Make a list or table to show the sorts of health problems that workers in these industries commonly suffer from.

3 Use the local library and newspapers to find out what the main industries are in your local area.

4 Using the information you have collected, draw conclusions (make suggestions) about the type of health problems people in your local area might suffer from.

Micro environments

Micro means small. In relation to your environment, micro means your personal environment or private space. It is easier to control a micro environment; one example might be a greenhouse, where the temperature, light and humidity (moistness of the atmosphere) are carefully controlled to provide the best environment for growing particular plants. Most indoor environments are micro environments because they are concerned with things that allow you to lead a healthy life, such as an indoor toilet and piped water supply. Furniture and fittings can also be considered part of the micro, or internal, environment.

Your micro environment is linked to your personal circumstances, for example, how much money you have and the sort of lifestyle you lead. This includes your home and the type of house you live in.

● ● ● *Housing*

In the UK, there are three main ways that you can obtain a home.

1   **Owner-occupier**
    This is when you borrow the money to buy a house from a bank or building society on a long-term loan, called a mortgage. You live in the property while you pay off the mortgage through regular payments. The amount of money that someone can borrow for a mortgage depends on how much money he or she earns, so it is usually only available to people in full-time, permanent employment. A mortgage is the most common form of home ownership in Britain, although it is less common in other parts of Europe. The owner-occupier is responsible for all maintenance and repairs to the property.

2   **Public housing**
    This is housing that is rented from either a local authority or a housing association. It is also called 'public sector housing'. It is intended for people who are unable to afford a mortgage or who have a housing need such as homelessness. Much less public sector housing has been built during the last twenty years, although it is on the rise again. This is because property is so expensive in some areas of the country, particularly London and the South East, that workers earning average or below average wages cannot afford a mortgage large enough to buy a home.

    Local authorities have a responsibility to house homeless and vulnerable people. Most local authorities, however, work in partnership with housing associations, which came into being in the 1980s. Much of the day-to-day responsibility for public housing now lies with these associations, including repairs and maintenance.

3   **Privately rented**
    This is where a person or organisation owns a property but allows someone

else to pay to live there. The owner is called the landlord and the person paying rent and living in the property is called the tenant. Some privately rented property is owned by organisations and some by individual landlords. The law gives protection to both landlords and tenants, setting out their rights and responsibilities through the Housing Act 1988 and its amendments. Landlords are responsible for the upkeep of the property and any repairs.

The amount of privately rented accommodation is increasing because there has been less public sector housing built in recent years. It is particularly common in large towns and cities, and where there are many students needing short-term accommodation. 14 per cent of the population and 55 per cent of students live in privately rented accommodation.

The condition of your home is likely to depend to some extent on whether you own or rent your property, how old the property is and whether it is maintained properly. Because buildings are affected by weather and age, the older the building the more likely it is to be in poor condition. If a building is erected using good quality materials and skilled workmen, it is likely to last longer and need fewer repairs, although it may be more expensive to buy.

• • • *Lifestyle and personal circumstances*

When we talk about lifestyle, we mean the way that people choose to live. Lifestyle includes not only where you live but also the sort of work you do and the health implications of this. It also includes what you eat and drink, whether you smoke and what activities you like to do in your spare time.

The sort of lifestyle you have will depend to some extent on how much money you have and the sort of choices that are available to you. The better lifestyle you are able to choose, the more control you will have over your personal environment and the healthier you are likely to be. Your lifestyle is closely linked to your personal circumstances. Therefore, a young, single person will have quite a different lifestyle to someone who has children. In addition, the sort of lifestyle you are able to have may change if your circumstances change.

One example is the financial effect of divorce. After divorce, the household's income will be significantly reduced. This will affect, for example, whether a mother has to return to full-time work in order to pay for housing and living expenses, such as food and heating, and childcare, to enable her to work. If she does, this change will in turn affect her lifestyle, from where she can live to the transport she can afford and the food her family can eat.

• • • *Leisure activities*

Leisure activities can range from dangerous or 'extreme' sports, such as bungee jumping or abseiling, to a leisurely walk around your local park. For most sports activities, you need to be trained by someone who is an expert and can show you how to prevent injuries.

CASE STUDY | leisure activities

Geoffrey lives in a village several miles from the local town. He enjoys going to the cinema and meeting friends for a meal afterwards. Unfortunately, the local bus service only runs from 7 a.m. until 9 p.m. and Geoffrey cannot afford to run a car on his wage. He therefore either has to go to the afternoon showing of a film or ask his friend from the town to give him a lift home. However, he does not like to do this because it means that his friend has a 10-mile round trip, which is a great inconvenience. For these reasons, Geoffrey's outings to the cinema are rare occasions. Mostly Geoffrey goes to the pub and plays darts in his time off.

D Suggest two ways in which Geoffrey could improve his lifestyle.

Types of internal environment

The internal environment is your personal environment where you spend most of your time. It includes those things that are directly important to you such as your immediate surroundings. Examples of internal environments are:

- home environment
- work environment
- recreational environment.

• • • *Home environment*

Although you have more control over your home environment, it is not regulated in the same way as the external environment. For example, you cannot be forced to have a smoke alarm fitted, even though it may prevent a fire. For this reason, the home has been called 'the most dangerous place' because more people suffer injuries, accidents or health problems there than anywhere else. Although the home is not regulated in the same way as public environments are, you do have a responsibility to visitors in your home.

However, if you rent your home there will be regulations that state your responsibilities for the safety of other tenants. This is because a rented home is seen as a public environment, since anyone can be a tenant. These regulations will cover different aspects of the home environment, such as fire resistant furniture coverings and the use and storage of poisonous substances such as bleach and cleaning products.

The home environment depends on the condition of the house or flat where you live, which in turn depends on your personal circumstances and lifestyle. Your health is affected directly and indirectly by the quality of your home. Houses in a poor state of repair often suffer from damp, which can cause mould to grow on the walls. If the house is inadequately heated and poorly ventilated, your health can be affected. For example, people living in these conditions can suffer from breathing conditions and chest infections.

• • • *Work environment*

There are various regulations concerned with the internal work environment, which is regulated under the Health and Safety at Work Act 1979. For example, the Act states which temperatures are considered unacceptable to work in and the required levels of heating, light and ventilation. Generally, temperatures should be between 13 and 16 degrees Celsius. If people's jobs require them to work in environments that are either very hot or cold, or outside, the employer must provide special clothing and facilities such as extra breaks. This Act also covers the responsibilities of employers for the health and safety of employees, and the responsibilities of employees for health and safety at work.

Many jobs can be hazardous to health because of the accidents or injuries that could happen. For example, if you work with a paper-cutting machine, there is a risk that you could accidentally cut yourself on the machine. Employees are also at risk from the materials and chemicals they handle at work. For example, smelting is an industrial process that turns raw materials such as copper and aluminium into copper wire for electrical cables or aluminium cans. Some of these processes bring workers into contact with acids or heavy metals that can affect the skin, nervous system, lungs or kidneys.

To ensure health and safety in the workplace, large organisations often have an occupational health department or service that employs specially trained and qualified doctors and nurses.

• • • *Recreational environment*

Activities that take place in teams, in leisure centres or in formal settings for sports activities are regulated because it is in the public interest. Other activities such as climbing, fell walking and cycling have sensible guidelines but individuals are not forced to follow these, even though it may be in their best interests.

• • • *Pets*

If you are an animal lover, pets can be good for your health. Pets provide company for people who are isolated and lonely, and stroking pets has been shown to lower blood pressure in people with hypertension (raised blood pressure). However, while pets are good for social and psychological health they can affect your physical health, e.g. by passing on fleas, bacteria and worms to humans. Some people are allergic to animals, and some pets can cause injury by biting, scratching, pecking, stinging or kicking.

Environmental hazards

Environmental hazards are those that pose a risk to human health from any aspect of the environment, external or internal.

- A hazard is a danger; something that causes harm.
- Risk is the likelihood of the harm occurring.

The risks from many of the hazards we face each day are reduced by government laws that control what organisations and individuals can and cannot do so that people are protected. For example, white-water rafting is a hazardous activity and accidents may occur. To reduce the risk of harm, if you want to do this activity you must go with a trained and experienced person, you must be able to swim, and you must wear the correct safety clothing, e.g. lifejackets and helmets. These precautions are intended to minimise the risk of drowning.

Types of hazards

Hazards can be physical, chemical, biological or social, and can relate to the external or internal environment.

Physical:
materials, structures, buildings, land, water or air that can cause physical harm.

Biological:
animals, micro-organisms, plants and other organisms that can cause physical harm.

Types of hazard

Chemical:
natural and man-made substances that can cause physical harm.

Social:
lifestyle and personal circumstances that can harm your social life, mental health and well-being.

The table on page 165 lists the four different types of hazards – physical, biological, chemical and social – and gives examples of each type for both external and internal environments.

Hazard	External examples	Internal examples
Physical	The condition of pavements, the volume of traffic, the quality of street lighting, litter and the condition of housing.	Faulty gas or electricity, furniture not meeting fire regulations, absence of a smoke alarm, inadequate heating, no hot water, draughts due to ill-fitting windows, worn carpets or dangerous floor coverings.
Biological	Vermin such as rats, mice, cockroaches, flying insects, bugs and lice; household pets or farm animals.	Bacterial infections such as gastro-enteritis caused by poor food hygiene and inadequate personal cleanliness.
Chemical	Herbicides, pesticides, fertilisers, traffic fumes and industrial pollution, e.g. incinerators.	Household chemicals such as cleaning products and air fresheners. Products must have labels on them to show whether they are toxic (damaging to health); many are packaged in special child-proof containers to reduce the likelihood of accidental poisoning.
Social	Social isolation, marital disharmony and domestic violence; bullying and harassment at work. Noise pollution is also a social health hazard.	Personal issues such as shyness and other communication difficulties.

GIVE IT A GO   environmental hazards

In pairs or small groups, visit your local supermarket, garden centre or hardware store. Examine the products used for pest control, cleaning or the garden. See if you can find any products labelled with the symbols below.

Write a brief report on each symbol to say:

▷ what the product is used for

▷ what the symbol means

▷ how to use and store the product

▷ what precautions you should take when using the product

▷ what to do if there is accidental misuse, e.g. spilling or swallowing the product.

• • • *Regulating environmental hazards*

All aspects of the macro environment are regulated to make sure that any risks to health are minimised. Within the external environment, hazards can come from land, water, air and waste. Any new risks, usually arising from scientific research, are assessed and regulations put into place to ensure the public are protected. Genetically modified (GM) food is one example of this.

Because these regulations are legal requirements, individuals or companies can be taken to court and punished if they fail to follow the rules and someone's health is damaged as a result. The main government department that deals with environmental matters is the Department of Environment, Food and Rural Affairs (DEFRA), www.defra.gov.uk.

Hazards in the macro environment

Hazards in the macro environment cover all aspects of the external environment – land, air and water.

● ● ● *Land use*

Land is used mainly for building and agriculture. Hazards to health can occur if the land is contaminated in some way by chemical or biological hazards.

● ● ● *Farming and agriculture*

Environmental hazards can be caused by farming methods. This is because farmers need to make the best use of their land, either for growing crops or for rearing animals, in order to make a living. The main types of environmental health hazards linked to farming and agriculture are chemical and biological hazards.

● ● ● *Chemical hazards*

Chemical hazards include:

● **Pesticides**
These are used to kill off insects and parasites that feed on the crops and spoil them. Pesticides also kill parasites on animals, for example, anthrax, which can be passed on to humans from sheep. Some pesticides are dangerous to humans so the Environmental Protection Act regulates the type and amount of pesticides that farmers can use.

● **Fertilisers**
These are used by farmers to increase the crop yield – the amount of crop produced from one sowing. Fertilisers contain nitrates, which can be washed into the water supply by the rain. If infant formula is made up with water containing high levels of nitrates, it can be harmful, causing a serious blood disorder called 'blue baby syndrome'. It is a very rare condition but nitrates must be kept at a low level in drinking water.

Spraying farm land with fertilisers.

Similar chemical fertilisers and pesticides are manufactured for use in domestic gardens. It is very important that chemicals are stored properly and according to instructions, and that you wash your hands after handling such chemicals.

• • • *Biological hazards*

Biological hazards include:

- **Animal faeces**
  Animal faeces contain bacteria called e-coli which can cause food poisoning. If you live on a farm or are planning to visit a farm, you need to take care to wash your hands thoroughly and keep your fingernails clean after handling animals.
- **Salmonella**
  This is a disease that is frequently present in chickens. You must thoroughly cook poultry and eggs before eating to destroy any salmonella bacteria.
- **Tuberculosis and brucellosis**
  These diseases are carried by cattle, although they are quite rare. Milk must be pasteurised during production to destroy these bacteria.

CASE STUDY identifying hazards

Sarah is the mother of 8-month-old Anna. They live in a small cottage on a farm where Sarah's husband, Terry, works as a farm labourer. Terry's main job is looking after the livestock and seeing to the chickens.

Anna has started to crawl and loves her new-found independence. Every night when Terry comes home, the first thing he does before he changes out of his work boots and clothes is pick Anna up from the floor and swing her in the air, which makes her squeal with delight.

Recently, Sarah has noticed a spotty, angry rash on Anna's face, neck and hands. She is concerned and contacts the health visitor. The health visitor prescribes some cream and the rash clears up.

1 What do you think might have caused Anna's rash?

2 What changes or precautions could Sarah and Terry take to identify the cause of the rash and prevent it recurring?

• • • *Building and development*

There is a great demand for buildings, not only because the population is increasing but because new homes are always needed to replace old properties. Homes wear out when building materials become less able to withstand the weather and their condition deteriorates.

Since most people now live in towns or cities, builders are being increasingly encouraged to re-use existing land. This is often previous industrial sites called 'brownfield sites'. However, this land may have been contaminated by chemicals or other forms of pollution as a result of industrial processes, and may be a health hazard. The site must therefore be cleaned up before building can start. Money is often available for urban regeneration through the European Union or government grants, to help with the cost of such specialised cleaning.

There are various chemical hazards linked to building and development, which are detailed below.

• • • *Asbestos*

Asbestos was often used as an insulating material. It is a particular problem because breathing in asbestos fibres and dust can cause cancer of the lungs. There are special rules for handling and disposing of asbestos.

• • • *Heavy metals*

Heavy metals are naturally occurring substances that are hazardous to health in low concentrations (low doses). These chemicals naturally occur on Earth, often deep below the surface, and are extracted by mining. They are used in many manufacturing processes and in industry, and are likely to contaminate brownfield sites. One of the problems with heavy metals is that they can accumulate and stay in your body for a long time. Workers in some manufacturing industries are exposed to these hazards and there are laws to protect them.

The most common heavy metals that are hazardous to health include:

- **Lead:** lead can affect your nervous system and brain function, causing loss of memory and lowered intelligence. It is particularly dangerous for children under 6 years of age and adolescents, because they are still growing. Lead is found in petrol products and paint. In some older properties, water pipes are made of lead.
- **Arsenic:** arsenic is used in the micro-electronics industry and as a wood preservative. Arsenic poisoning can affect the skin and high doses can cause death. It also causes lung cancer.
- **Mercury:** mercury is found in thermometers and gauges, although it is gradually being replaced in the health care industry with electronic or digital equipment. Mercury is also used in batteries, to fill teeth (amalgam) and in the mining of gold and silver. Too much mercury can damage the kidneys and nervous system.
- **Cadmium:** this metal is one of the main substances found in batteries and industrial paints, particularly car paint. If you inhale it when sprayed, you can die from breathing difficulties.

• • • *Food*

The food you eat is carefully regulated in all stages of production – literally from farm to table. Overall responsibility for food lies with the Food Standards Agency (www.food.gov.uk), which advises the government on food production.

• • • *Meat*

The health and treatment of animals for food production is monitored by vets.

Animal welfare and feed, and the way animals are transported, killed and prepared for food, are all monitored and inspected by vets and environmental health officers to ensure safety. Despite these checks, environmental hazards have been associated with meat, particularly in relation to BSE and the human illness that it causes. Many changes have been made since it was discovered that animal feed affects both the health of the animals and the humans who eat the animals.

• • • *Fruit and vegetables*

For fruit and vegetables, food regulations are mainly concerned with pesticide traces that remain after picking. The Food Standards Agency monitors food to make sure that it is not contaminated, carries out research on the health implications of food production, and checks nutritional standards. It also advises on healthy eating for the population as a whole.

Environmental health officers from the local authority monitor standards of hygiene in shops and restaurants where food is sold.

• • • *Air quality*

In recent years, governments have become increasingly worried about the effects of worldwide environmental pollution. A particular concern is atmospheric pollution, which has been destroying the ozone layer in the earth's atmosphere.

- **Aerosol sprays**
  These have been found to damage the ozone layer due to the propellant gases (CFCs) which make them squirt from the spray can. This is an example of a chemical hazard. The ozone layer protects people from the harmful effects of the sun's radiation, which causes skin cancer. Because of the damage to the ozone layer, it is estimated that the number of people suffering from skin cancer (malignant melanoma) will rise. According to Cancer Research, skin cancer rates have increased faster than any other major cancer since the 1970s.
- **Fossil fuels**
  Fossil fuels are coal, oil, gas and wood. These cause atmospheric pollution when they are burned for heating and cooking.

- **Traffic**

One of the major causes of atmospheric pollution is the huge increase in traffic, especially in cars and aeroplanes, which both need fuel derived from fossil fuels to operate (petrol is a by-product of oil, and diesel is a by-product of gas). Traffic poses both a physical hazard and a chemical hazard. Vehicle exhaust fumes send tiny solid particles of matter into the air that can affect your lungs when inhaled and cause asthma. The chemicals in the particles also mix with moisture in the atmosphere to form acids. When this falls as rain, it turns lakes and rivers acidic, affecting fish and wildlife. Acid rain also eats away at brick and stonework, causing buildings to decay more rapidly.

- **Industrial processes**

Air pollution from heavy industry.

These contribute to air pollution when the by-products of production are discharged into the atmosphere. The extent to which these pollutants are dispersed often depends on the weather: if there is low cloud, for example, the substances are not dispersed very quickly. Also, the action of sunlight on some by-products can change them into more dangerous pollutants. The countries of the European Union have an agreement on air quality and how this is to be monitored. The responsibility for monitoring local industry for air pollution lies with local authorities.

• • • *Water quality*

The lack of access to clean, safe drinking water is one of the main causes of ill health across the globe. In the UK, however, almost everyone now has access to clean water from a tap in his or her home.

• • • *Water quality in the UK*

Water in the UK is provided by companies that were created in 1989 by the privatisation of ten publicly-owned regional water authorities that provided both water and sewage services. The government through the Department for Environment, Food and Rural Affairs (DEFRA) monitors the quality of drinking water and makes sure that water companies abide by the regulations for drinking water. Sewage treatment has improved and it is now illegal to discharge raw (untreated) sewage into the sea.

In addition, the National Rivers Authority monitors the quality of water and extent of pollution in rivers and streams from sewage and agriculture. Water standards are inspected and monitored by the Environment Agency (www.environment-agency.gov.uk) and the Drinking Water Inspectorate (www.dwi.gov.uk) on behalf of DEFRA.

• • • *River pollution*

River water can be polluted by:

- Chemicals from farming, for example, nitrates found in fertilisers can damage rivers and streams by increasing the amount of weeds and algae. These use up oxygen in the water and this affects the ability of fish to breed and survive.
- Bacteria or parasites from animals, for example, cryptosporidium is a parasite that causes diarrhoea.

Hazards in the micro environment

Hazards in the micro or internal environment include those at home and work.

• • • *Hazards in the home*

There are many hazards in the home environment and almost all of them are avoidable.

• • • *Damp and cold conditions*

These cause mould to grow, releasing tiny spores that are invisible to the naked eye. When people breathe in the mould spores, it can cause repeated chest infections and asthma, particularly in children and older people. Conditions such as arthritis and rheumatism, which cause the joints to become stiff and painful, can also become worse.

• • • *Inadequate heating*

Many people do not have central heating and rely on gas or, less commonly, electric fires to heat their homes. Gas fires need regular servicing and maintenance to check that they work properly. If they are faulty, dangerous carbon monoxide fumes can build up in the atmosphere causing carbon monoxide poisoning. Carbon monoxide does not smell and cannot easily be detected, but it can be fatal because it stops you breathing in oxygen. The Housing Act 1988 states that landlords have a responsibility to check all gas appliances and issue a safety certificate before they can let a property. Despite this, ten students in privately rented accommodation have died from carbon monoxide poisoning since 1990.

• • • *Electrical hazards*

If the electrical wiring system in a house has been badly installed or is in a poor state of repair, for example, because of age, it becomes a fire risk. Faulty wiring and overloading of electric sockets is one of the most common causes of house fires. It is estimated that you are six times more likely to die in a fire if you live in a bed-sit. Smoke alarms can help save lives by warning of a fire and giving you time to escape.

••• *Household dust*

Dust mites are tiny invisible creatures that live in soft furnishings, bedding and carpets. If you are allergic to the house dust mite, it can cause asthma and eczema. It is not possible to prevent the house dust mite; however, regular vacuuming of carpets and dusting with a damp cloth to prevent dust flying into the air can be helpful. It is also possible to buy special mattresses and pillows that discourage the mites.

••• *Lead pipes*

The responsibility of water companies for the water supply only extends to the boundary of the property. Owners or landlords are responsible for the pipes that supply water into the house. In older properties, these pipes are sometimes made from lead; in areas of the country where the water naturally contains calcium, this can cause the lead to dissolve slightly and contaminate the water. Lead is known to affect the brain and central nervous system in large quantities and is particularly dangerous for children. Because of this, lead in paint has been banned for many years.

••• *Hazards at work*

If you work in an office, it is important to get your eyes tested regularly because computer screens can affect your vision. Your employer should pay for an eye test for you if you spend most of your working day at a computer. It is also important that you have a chair that supports your body properly. Another common health problem is repetitive strain injury (RSI) which is caused by regular typing. RSI is a very painful condition that affects your ability to use your hands, although it improves with rest.

••• *Lifestyle hazards*

One example of a lifestyle hazard is pets.

- Some people are allergic to pet fur or feathers and this can cause asthma, especially in children.
- Dogs, especially pregnant bitches and puppies, can be infested with roundworms and these can be passed on to children. If the soil in parks and gardens becomes contaminated by animal faeces from dogs, children may get the worm eggs on their fingers and under their nails. If they then put their fingers in their mouth, the eggs will be swallowed and the worms will hatch, causing toxocariasis.
- Pregnant women should not handle cat litter as cats may be infected with a parasite that causes toxoplasmosis. This disease is mild in adults, causing symptoms similar to influenza. However, the infection can be passed to the developing baby causing serious abnormalities.

Investigating an environmental issue

The environmental issue you choose to investigate can be either an external or internal issue that is causing or is likely to cause a health problem. If you choose an external issue, you will need some knowledge of your local area. If you choose an internal issue, you will need to have access to the home of someone you know quite well and seek his or her permission to carry out the investigation. If you discover a risk to people's health through your investigation, you will need to make sure that the people involved know what action to take to protect themselves and have access to accurate information. You should discuss these issues further with your tutor.

Identifying a relevant issue

• • • *Finding out about your local area*

In order to understand what health issues might be relevant to the population in your local area, you need to be able to identify the boundaries of your area. There are different ways of working this out. Below are some different methods you might use.

- **By electoral ward:** each local authority area is divided into smaller areas known as electoral wards. Each of these smaller areas has a councillor who is elected to represent people of that ward on the local council.
- **By GP practice area:** most GPs (doctors known as general practitioners) will look after around 2000 patients, and the area they cover will depend on the number of people living there. For example, a GP working in a town or city may only cover two or three miles, whereas in rural areas a GP's practice area may cover twenty miles.
- **By postcode:** the areas covered by postcodes vary in size and may contain a wide variety of environments, having very different issues.
- **By local name:** most towns have named local areas that may be familiar to you and that could be used for your study. It is important that you describe clearly where such local areas begin and end.

GIVE IT A GO discovering your local area

In groups of two or three, visit your local library or town hall. Find out how the local area is divided into electoral wards and which areas are covered by GP practices. See if you can obtain a map and draw on it the boundaries you have identified.

1 Is your area urban, suburban, industrial or rural?

2 Identify the poorest and the least poor areas.

3 What are the local industries?

You should discuss with your tutor the most useful method of choosing the locality that you wish to study.

• • • *Links to health, safety and well-being*

In order to work out the likely risks to people's health in your local area, you need to know something about who the population is, e.g. whether there are more older people in the area or whether the area has a lot of families with young children. You may have local knowledge yourself but, if not, clues can be found by counting the number of schools and nurseries (which would suggest how many children are in the locality). Similarly, if there are many residential homes or sheltered accommodation in the area, there is likely to be a larger than average number of older people.

The main characteristics of a particular population can be identified by counting the number of people in different age groups. This is known as a population profile. The whole population of England and Wales is counted every few years through the census. The results are published and made available through libraries and on the Internet.

The level of risk posed by a particular hazard will vary, depending on the vulnerability of the individual person. For example:

- **Elderly people** tend to be more at risk of illness and infection because their immune systems are not as efficient and therefore their resistance to disease is reduced. They are also more at risk of falls because they are often not as mobile and their muscles and joints are weaker than in younger adults. Chest infections are particularly common in older people because they do not exercise their lungs and may have smoked when younger, reducing their lung capacity.
- **Children** are more at risk than adults because of their small size: any poisonous or harmful substances such as chemicals or toxins will affect them in smaller amounts. In addition, because children are growing and continuing to develop, some substances can disrupt normal development and growth.
- **Pregnant women** are vulnerable because of their unborn babies. Some substances and products can be hazardous to the developing baby, causing infections to the mother and abnormalities in the baby.

Investigating the issue

When investigating your environmental issue, you will need to carry out an environmental survey.

• • • *Macro environments*

If you are looking at a macro environmental issue, this means that you will need a picture of the area you intend to study. This includes:

- A map of the area. This can be one you have drawn or part of a published map.

The boundaries of the area you have chosen to study need to be clearly marked.

- Photographs of the particular area you will be studying. You can either take these yourself or contact the local newspaper office to see if they have any. You may also find some pictures in the library, but sometimes you have to pay to use these.

● ● ● *Micro environments*

If you intend to study an internal environment, you will need:

- A floor plan of the rooms. If possible, you should draw these on graph paper. It is helpful if they are drawn to scale (an accurate miniature version).
- Photographs of the environment. You are likely to have to take these yourself.

▢▢▢ EVIDENCE ACTIVITY

Environmental survey

1 Walk around the area, including any side streets. Make notes and, if possible, take some pictures of what you see.

2 Write up your impressions, describing the physical condition of the area, e.g. pavements, streetlights, litter, etc.

3 Give a presentation to the rest of the class. Include as much detail as possible about your impression of the area, for example, the most common type of housing and traffic, and the general condition of the area.

Exploring the effects of the environmental issue

It is important to be aware that even common activities can be a health hazard to some people, who may be more vulnerable.

One example is chlorine in swimming pools, which is used to prevent infection and keep the water clean. It is thought that when chlorine mixes with body fluids such as urine, it forms a dangerous gas that can bring on asthmatic attacks. It is also thought that this same process causes redness and stinging of the eyes, a common after-effect of swimming. The level of risk depends on the amount of chlorine in the water (which is regulated by law), the number of people swimming and the personal hygiene of the swimmers. This is why it is important to shower before entering the water. The authorities are looking at other substances they might use instead of chlorine. Another potential hazard from swimming pools is cryptosporidium, which is a parasite causing stomach upsets with vomiting and diarrhoea.

◼◼◼ EVIDENCE ACTIVITY

Identifying health risks

1 **Find out what health problems can be caused by:**
   ▷ traffic pollution
   ▷ computer screens (visual display units, or VDUs)
   ▷ household chemicals such as bleach and washing soda crystals
   ▷ vermin such as rats, mice or cockroaches.

2 **Say which groups of people are most at risk from the health problems you have identified and why they are at greater risk.**

• • • Health and safety issues

It is important that you can identify how the issue you have identified is likely to affect the health of individuals and specific groups of people, both in the short-term and in the long-term.

CASE STUDY external [macro] environmental issue

Chempro/Unifix is a specialist waste disposal company. They have applied to the local council for planning permission to build an incinerator to process industrial waste on the site of an old electricity power station by the river. The power station was situated 1.5 kilometres from the town centre on the main road leading to the next town; however, it has been closed for over fifteen years. Further along the main road is a village that has become an attractive place to live for young professionals – it is in open countryside but within reach of local towns and the motorway network. New housing has been built and there are plans to expand the local primary school. The village residents are strongly opposed to the plans for the incinerator and are planning a campaign to stop it.

1 Give details of one short-term and one long-term health hazard to particular individuals or groups in the village arising from these plans.

2 Who will be responsible for regulating the company?

3 What are the benefits to the environment of building the incinerator?

CASE STUDY internal [micro] environmental issue

Mrs Elizabeth Whittle is a 75-year-old widow who lives alone in the home she used to share with her husband and family. The house is a three-bedroom semi-detached property on the outskirts of town. The house has central heating; however, Mrs Whittle only has it on in the living room and bathroom because it is expensive. She has recently noticed that the wallpaper in the corner of her bedroom is peeling from the wall; black mould is growing behind it and the wall feels damp. Mrs Whittle wipes the mould off every day where she can reach it.

1   What might be causing the mould?

2   How might this affect Mrs Whittle's health?

3   What action could she take in the short-term?

4   What action could she consider in the long-term to reduce these health hazards?

Raising awareness of environmental issues

The role of local authorities

The government has passed some of the day-to-day responsibilities for looking after the health, safety and well-being of local communities, including those concerned with the environment, to local authorities (your local council). Local authorities both provide services and check to see if regulations are being observed through a department of environmental services.

● ● ● *Environmental health officers*

Specially trained people called environmental health officers carry out monitoring activities to ensure that laws are not broken. They have the power to take offenders to court or impose fines if the law is being broken.

● ● ● *Local environmental services*

Services provided by local authorities that are concerned with the environment include:

- public housing, e.g. council housing or housing association property
- street cleaning and lighting
- roads and pavements
- recreation and leisure, e.g. parks, swimming pools, playing fields
- traffic management, e.g. parking and traffic calming schemes

- recycling, waste collection and disposal
- food and hygiene regulations relating to the sale and preparation of food
- systems for monitoring industrial pollution.

Many of these services are paid for by the population through council tax. The government also gives money to the local authorities for services. In some cases, the local authority will draw-up a contract with other organisations to provide services on their behalf. One example of this is the collection of household waste.

⬤⬤⬤ EVIDENCE ACTIVITY

Local authority services

1 Find out what services the local authority provides in the area you have chosen to study.

2 Are these services provided by the local authority directly or does another company provide them on behalf of the local authority?

Sources of information

As part of your investigation, it is important that you know and understand where to get information on your environmental issue. In order to raise awareness of the environmental problem you have identified, you must provide information and advice for people and make it available to them.

- Your local council will have an environment department that you could contact to ask for information; they are also likely to employ Environmental Health Officers who may be able to give you local information (your tutor may even be able to arrange for such a person to give a talk to your group).
- Information about environmental hazards often makes newspaper headlines so you could contact your local paper.
- The library is a good source of information, as is the Internet.
- Extensive information is provided by the Department of the Environment, Food and Rural Affairs (www.defra.gov.uk).
- Information on health issues can often be obtained from your local health centre, as well as health professionals such as health visitors and district nurses.
- If your environmental issue is likely to affect a particular group of people, you may be able to contact charities such as Age Concern or Disability Action in your local area.

◨◨◨ EVIDENCE ACTIVITY

Sources of information

1 Make a poster to highlight the health effects of your chosen issue. The poster should include:

   ▷ where people can obtain information, e.g. the Department of the Environment, Food and Rural Affairs or the local authority;

   ▷ where people can get help to solve the environmental problem, e.g. replacing lead water pipes;

   ▷ where to go for help with environmental health issues.

2 Where would you display your poster to reach the people most likely to be affected?

● ● ● *Scope for improvement*

When considering how the environment could be improved, you will need to think about:

- What environmental regulations apply to this area?
- Who is responsible for monitoring and regulating the environment?
- What could individuals or groups do to improve the environment in this area?

There are several ways in which local people can bring environmental issues to the attention of the authorities. These include:

- writing to your local member of parliament (MP) – you will need to find out who he or she is
- contacting the local newspaper or radio station – you could write an article for publication
- bringing the issue to the attention of healthcare professionals so that they can forward the issue through their professional organisations – you will need to find out who these are.

unit 7

Looking after children

In this unit you will learn about the growth and development of children. You will look at the different ways that children learn and discover the importance of communicating with babies and young children to promote their learning.

You will investigate how to meet children's individual needs by providing for their safety, providing love, affection, patience and understanding.

You will discover why children need exercise, sleep, food and good hygiene to keep physically healthy.

In this unit you will learn about:

- how children grow and develop
- how children learn
- what children need
- how to keep children physically healthy.

How children grow and develop

Growth and development

In order for a helpless baby to turn into a capable adult the body needs to grow and develop. When we talk of *growth* we are really describing an increase in size. *Development*, on the other hand, describes the increasing skills and abilities as the child matures.

● ● ● *Growth*

Babies and young children are regularly weighed and measured to check their growth and progress. At birth the average measurements are as follows:

- Weight   3.5 kgs
- Head circumference (measurement round head)   34 cm
- Length   50 cm

The rate of growth is not the same throughout life. The greatest period of growth happens between birth and 2 years.

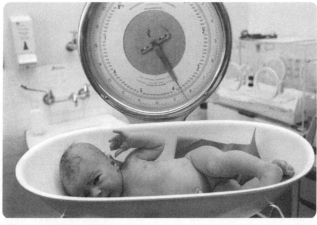

Weighing a baby at birth.

How the body shape changes from infancy to adulthood.

● ● ● *Size and shape*

You can see in the chart opposite how the child's body shape changes over time.

● ● ● *Weight*

Did you know that a baby doubles his or her weight in the first 6 months of life? A baby trebles in weight by the age of 1 year and by 2 years weighs four times as much as the day he or she was born. By the time the child is 7 years old, he or she may be seven times heavier than at birth.

GIVE IT A GO — comparisons

The circumference of a baby's head is about the same size or larger than the chest measurement. Now compare your head to your chest measurement and see the difference.

••• *Bones*

As the baby grows the bones in his or her body increase in number as well as size. The bones also become harder so that they are strong enough to support the baby when he or she is ready to stand and walk.

••• *Muscles*

The muscles have to grow and gain strength to support the body and to control movement. Tiny babies are floppy and cannot hold up their heads or sit up until the muscles grow in size and strength.

GIVE IT A GO — growth

If you know someone with a baby or young child, ask if you can see his or her growth chart.

••• *Development*

As the nervous system (the brain, the spinal cord and the nerves) develop, the baby gains more control of his or her muscles and develops greater skills. As the brain develops so the child's understanding improves and he or she learns to think and work things out independently.

CASE STUDY — growth and development

Daisy was 3.5 kg when she was born. She had little control as she waved her arms and hands about. As she got older her hands got bigger and became more skilful. By about 9 months of age she could hold a spoon and bash it about in her plate of dinner; by 15 months of age she had enough control and strength in her hands and wrist to load the spoon with custard and place most of it in her mouth. By the age of 4 years her hands were big enough to control a knife and fork.

▷ Find an example of Daisy's growth.

▷ Find an example of her development.

▷ What might Daisy's weight be at the age of (a) 6 months and (b) 1 year?

●●● EVIDENCE ACTIVITY

Growth and development

Write a brief description of a child's life between the age of birth and 2 years. Describe his or her growth and development during this time. If you know a young baby, talk to the mother to help you with this work.

Developmental expectations in infancy and early childhood

A developmental expectation or milestone is the average age at which a child achieves a particular skill. For example, the developmental expectation, or average age, for a child to learn to walk is 13 months. Although Richard walked at 10 months and Bridget did not walk until 15 months, both children are within normal developmental limits.

●●● *Areas of development*

Development is usually divided into four different areas: physical, social, emotional, intellectual. Some milestones in these four areas of development are given in the table below. Remember, these are the *average* ages at which the child develops these skills.

Age	Physical skills	Social skills	Emotional skills	Intellectual skills
0–3 months	Plays with fingers, can lift head and chest	Smiles	Dependent on others	Uses senses to explore
6 months	Rolls from back to tummy, sits with support, grasps rattle	May be scared of strangers	Upset if mother leaves	Watches adults and tries to copy them
9 months	Sits alone, may crawl, picks up small objects	Shy with strangers, enjoys 'peek a boo' and clapping	Gets angry easily, shows fear of loud noises	Looks for a toy that has fallen from the pram
12 months	May stand alone, walks round furniture	Waves bye-bye	Likes to be close to familiar adult, demonstrates affection	Learns to say a few words
18 months	Walks confidently, builds a tower of two bricks, uses crayons to scribble	Copies domestic tasks, plays alone but likes to be near a familiar adult	Wants to do things for him or herself	Short concentration span

Age	Physical skills	Social skills	Emotional skills	Intellectual skills
2 years	Climbs on furniture, walks on tiptoe, builds tower with six bricks	Plays near others and may copy them	Has tantrums when frustrated, may be jealous of others	Can use shape sorter or very simple jigsaw, learns simple rhymes
3 years	Enjoys jumping, kicks a ball, rides a tricycle, threads large beads, uses scissors	Plays with other children, begins to understand sharing and taking turns	Shows affection to younger children	Knows name of some colours, completes jigsaws with more pieces
4 years	Runs and climbs, can kick and throw a ball, threads small beads, can draw a person	Plays more complex games with other children, understands sharing	More independent, more confident	Improved concentration, can count to ten, learns names of shapes
5 years	Can skip and hop, runs well, can thread large needle, good control when writing	Chooses friends, begins to understand rules	Keen to do well, shows sympathy to friends	Starts to learn to read
8 years	Rides a bike well, draws detailed drawings	Friends are very important, often has a close friend of own sex	Quite independent	Thinks in a more complex way

CASE STUDY areas of development

- Vlada can count to ten.
- Mark's best friend is Toby.
- Ravi can roll onto his tummy.
- Jamila is having a tantrum.
- Jessica is able to take turns riding the tricycle.

1. How old are each of these children?
2. What area of development is described?

How children learn

Learning through exploration

Young children learn by exploring using all their senses – sight, hearing, touch, taste and smell. The mouth is the most sensitive part of the body, so everything that a baby picks up will be put in his or her mouth. This means that it is really important that toys for young babies are clean and have no small pieces they could choke on.

CASE STUDY using the senses

Shabana is exploring her new play mat. She looks at all the different colours and shapes, then she pokes a big yellow sun and it squeaks. She does it again and chuckles. Her fingers slide onto a furry lamb and she likes the feel, so she opens and closes her hand letting her fingers play with the material. There is a bone ring attached to the mat with a short ribbon. Her fingers fasten round the ring and she puts it in her mouth. It is lovely and cool on her gums. It is too big to get the whole ring into her mouth, however hard she tries. The mat is comfortable and smells of her mother. Shabana feels safe.

▷ List all the different senses Shabana uses as she explores her new toy.

▷ How do you know that this is a safe toy for Shabana?

CASE STUDY exploring the environment

1 year-old Jamie has a shape sorter, a teddy and a toddle truck to play with while his mum does the ironing. Jamie is bored of putting the shapes into the holes in the shape sorter. He has found that he can fit a brick into the hole in the video machine, which is much more fun. He is tired of his teddy so he tries to cuddle the cat, which runs away. Jamie pulls himself up to standing and although he has a toddle truck, he has much more fun walking round the furniture. He has a little chew of the material on the seat of the sofa. Then he takes hold of the side of a table as he tries to reach a cup of tea. The table falls over and the cup of tea makes a big wet mark on the carpet.

▷ Why is Jamie using the environment instead of his toys?

▷ What skills is Jamie learning as he explores his environment?

▷ Can you find some other exciting things that Jamie might explore in this room?

• • • *Safety issues*

When children explore their environment, adults are responsible for making sure that they are safe.

WHAT if Safety in the environment

...*You were asked to look after a 1-year-old baby?*

▷ Make a list of all the dangers you can see in the illustration of Jamie on page 185.

▷ Describe what you would do to keep Jamie safe.

Windows — secure so that no child can fall out; made with unbreakable glass

Floors — clean, dry and clear of objects the child could fall over

Doors that will not slam shut or trap fingers

Safety inside

Stairs protected so a child can't fall down them

Kitchens — no access to sharp knives or hot cookers

Toilets — clean; high lock on door so that child can't lock him or herself in; medicines locked away or kept out of reach

---

Surfaces — safe, i.e. round play equipment, no animal droppings

Plants — no poisonous plants

Gates and fences — locked and secure

Safety outside

Dustbins and rubbish — out of reach of children

Water — no access to water

Equipment — not rusty or broken; play is supervised

Sun — shade and protection from the full sun

GIVE IT A GO   safety in the environment

Look at your living room and kitchen. List all the things you would have to do to make these environments safe if a 2-year-old baby was coming to stay.

As children's skills develop, they have different safety needs so you should understand what behaviour to expect from children at different ages. This is important in order to protect children and prevent accidents. The chart below describes the skills children achieve and the hazards they face at different ages.

Age	Expected behaviour	Hazards when exploring
6–9 months	Learns to roll over, can move round floor by crawling or shuffling, can pick up objects, begins to feed him or herself, explores through the senses	May fall off surfaces if left unattended, can reach unprotected areas, may put small objects in mouth, may choke if left unattended
12–18 months	Learns to walk and begins to climb, can hold smaller objects, increased curiosity	Can get into unsafe places, e.g. kitchen, stairs, toilet, and climb on furniture, puts small things in mouth
18 months– 3 years	Learns to run and jump, can turn door handles, curious about environment and keen to explore	Enjoys climbing on things and jumping off, no sense of danger so may fall, can leave a room and find dangerous places
3–5 years	Can run fast, jump and hop, has good sense of balance and can ride a tricycle, threads beads, less likely to put things in the mouth but should not be left unsupervised	Falls from heights and tricycles, may put small objects in nose or ears
5–8 years	Increased physical skills, e.g. climbing, swinging and riding a bicycle; influenced by friends	Climbing and riding accidents, may be easily led into danger by others

GIVE IT A GO   safety outside

▷ List all the dangerous features in this park.

▷ What age of child would you allow to play on each piece of equipment?

▷ Take a walk round your local park to see how safe it is.

Learning through play

There are lots of definitions of the word 'play'. Many people think that play describes the experiences that children have when they have chosen what to do. Children play in different ways at different stages of their development.

• • • *Play at different ages*

0–2 years	Solitary play	Babies and toddlers spend a lot of time playing happily on their own.
2–3 years	Parallel play	Children are beginning to notice what other children do, and may play alongside others, often copying what they do.
3–5 years	Simple co-operative play	By now children begin to be able to share and take turns, so are able to join in simple group games and activities.
5–8 years	Complex co-operative play	Children are now able to make up complex games that often go on for days. They can make up their own rules and organise themselves.

CASE STUDY stages of play

You have glanced through the window at the parent and toddler group. Decide what stage of play these children are at:

▢ Jo and Nathan are playing with a cardboard box, pretending it is a car. They take turns to climb inside and be the driver.

▢ Erin is on her own on the mat, stacking up a pile of bricks.

▢ Farhan, Joel and Lisa are playing monsters. Joel tells Farhan he must hide under the climbing frame. He tells Lisa to go into the corner and count to ten before coming to look for them.

▢ Janine and Jason are at the dough table. Jason is copying Janine as she rolls out a long sausage of dough.

••• *Types of play to encourage different skills*

Children need to explore a wide range of different types of play.

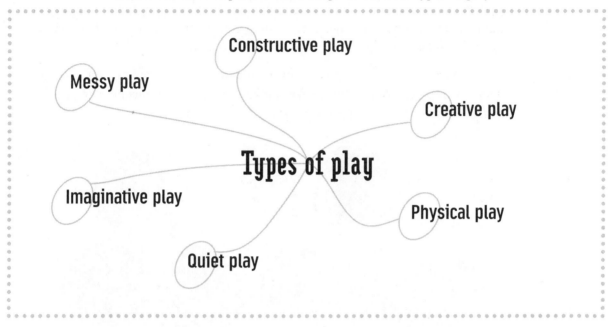

••• *Messy play*

Children get great pleasure using their senses to explore and experiment with sand and water. They discover that dry sand and water will pour through a funnel, but wet sand will not. It is also very soothing for children to run their fingers through dry sand or warm water. In addition, children learn to share buckets and spades. They learn fine manipulative skills (use of the hands and fingers) and hand–eye coordination as they pour water into jugs or build roads and tunnels in the sand.

••• *Constructive play*

All children enjoy building things. Can you remember at what age a child can build a tower of six bricks? During constructive play, children learn fine motor skills and hand–eye coordination. They learn to work with others and to solve problems. It is important to provide a range of different construction toys for children at different ages.

GIVE IT A GO construction resources

Find a toy catalogue or visit a toy shop and find four different construction kits that you could give to children at different ages.

• • • *Creative play and early writing opportunities*

The first stage of writing happens when a baby, for example, plays with his or her pudding and notices that by moving his or her fingers through the food, marks are made. Drawing and painting activities help children to develop the fine motor skills and hand–eye coordination which are essential for writing.

Children can express their feelings through painting and drawing and making collages. They will learn about colour, texture and shape while enjoying the satisfaction of creating their own work.

Children engaged in creative play.

GIVE IT A GO creative play

Using the following resources, create a picture or model:

▷ Cut a potato in half and carve a pattern on the cut surface. Using some children's paint, create a pattern picture.

▷ Find many different blue materials (e.g. paper, wool material, sequins) and create a 'blue' picture.

• • • *Imaginative play*

Role play encourages children to use their imagination. We know that they like to copy what adults do, so play in a home corner is an ideal opportunity to practise being 'grown up'; for example, to experience domestic tasks and pretend to be different people. Children can dress up as nurses, doctors, police officers, fire officers or chefs.

GIVE IT A GO   role play resources

Get hold of a toy catalogue or visit a toyshop and find examples of the following role play resources, which encourage children to value diversity:

▷ cooking utensils such as woks and chapatti pans

▷ play food from different cultures

▷ dolls and puppets with different skin tones

▷ dressing-up clothes from different cultures.

• • • *Physical play*

During this type of play, children develop large motor skills (use of their body, arms and legs) and fine motor skills (use of their hands and fingers). Physical play is also important for children's health and well-being as it strengthens bones and muscles, improves the appetite and encourages good sleep patterns.

GIVE IT A GO   physical exercise

▷ Make a list of all the physical activities you and your friends enjoy.

▷ Do you think that you take enough exercise?

• • • *Quiet play*

Quiet play describes the quiet and gentle activities that are so important for young children. One of the most important quiet activities involves sharing books and stories with children. Sometimes sharing a quiet board game or having a discussion can be quite relaxing.

▢▢▢ EVIDENCE ACTIVITY

Types of play

Prepare a booklet you could give to a parent to help them understand how different types of play help children's learning and development.

Learning by example

We can all learn by example through watching other people. Sometimes this happens formally and sometimes informally.

• • • *Formal learning*

You may find that when your teacher wants to teach you some new skill, he or she will show you what to do before you are asked to practise the new skill.

• • • *Informal learning*

Children are always watching other people and copying what they do. A tiny baby will copy an adult who puts out his or her tongue. A toddler will copy his mother as she dusts the living room or sweeps the floor. A mum will complain when her 6-year-old daughter comes home from school and uses a swear word that she learnt in the playground.

GIVE IT A GO learning by example

Can you think of something you have learnt by watching others:

▷ formally

▷ informally?

• • • *Providing good role models*

Young children copy the attitudes and behaviour of the people they admire. For this reason, you must be a good role model because young children will imitate you.

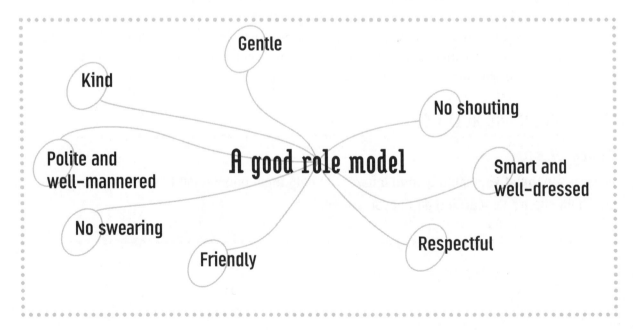

• • • *Allowing children to explore gender roles*

Some people think that girls should play with dolls, tea sets and dressing-up clothes, and that boys should play with footballs, cars and science toys. These ideas limit opportunities for boys and girls alike. You must therefore encourage both boys and girls to play with all the toys in the setting.

WHAT if   **Exploring gender roles**

...*You wanted to challenge gender roles?*

You work at Tree Tops Nursery and you have noticed that most of the girls play in the home corner while the boys play at pirates on the climbing frame.

▷ What would you do in this situation?

• • • *Recognising and making provision for diversity*

We live in a multicultural society where people from different cultural and racial backgrounds have different life experiences and expectations. It is important that people working with children value and respect the fact that everyone is different and has different needs. After all, if you went into a restaurant and everyone was given the same meal, you would not be very happy. A good restaurant provides a wide range of food so that everyone can choose the meal that suits them the best. In the same way, you too must provide resources and experiences to meet the needs of all the different families in society.

Diversity in the environment

- 'Welcome' notices in different languages
- Books and stories with images of different types of family
- Home corner resources from different cultures
- Musical instruments from different cultures
- Dressing-up clothes that reflect different styles of dress
- Dolls and puppets with different skin tones

To provide a welcoming and diverse environment, people need to see things that they feel familiar with.

Communication

Through communication, young children learn to understand the meaning of all the things they discover in their environment. Communication is not just about talking but includes: listening, speaking, reading and writing.

• • • *The importance of talking to babies and young children*

Babies need adults to listen and talk to them in order to help with all areas of their development.

Area of development	Use of language to support learning
Physical (relating to the body)	To describe movements and parts of the body; to tell people what they need.
Intellectual (relating to the mind)	To understand concepts such as colour, size, shape, weight, number, etc.
Emotional (relating to the feelings)	To talk about feelings; to express anger, jealously, fear, etc.
Social (relating to other people)	To make friends; to communicate and share experiences with other people.

CASE STUDY communication with young children

▷ One-year-old Javaria is crying. She calms down when she hears her mum singing quietly to comfort her.

▷ Two-year-old Caroline tells her mother she wants a drink.

▷ Three-year-old Imran is learning the names of the different colours.

▷ Four-year-old Melissa plays with her friends in the home corner. She tells the others that they must come and get their tea.

▷ Five-year-old Steven is frightened about going to the dentist. His mum reads him a story about a trip to the dentist.

▷ Six-year-old Jason is learning to write. On Mondays he writes a story about what he did at the weekend which he then shares with his class.

1 Find an example of these different types of communication: listening, speaking, reading, writing.

2 Find an example of using language to support:
   ▷ physical development
   ▷ emotional development
   ▷ intellectual development
   ▷ social development.

• • • *How babies and young children communicate*

There are two distinct ways that we all communicate:

- verbal communication – using words and sentences
- non-verbal communication – using facial expressions and body movements.

GIVE IT A GO non-verbal communication

Everybody communicates without words. You may sometimes look cross and sulky, or happy and excited. Work with another student and share the following information without using words:

☐ you want a drink   ☐ you are angry

☐ you are tired   ☐ goodbye.

CASE STUDY babies communicating

You might think that a baby who cannot speak cannot communicate. This is not at all true: babies communicate in many different ways. What do you think these babies are telling you?

• • • *Listening to children*

In order to communicate well with children it is very important that you are able to listen and understand what children need. Some guidelines for listening to children are:

- Sit down so that you are level with them.
- Watch their eyes, facial expression and body movements.

- Pay attention.
- Give them time to finish their sentences.

CASE STUDY listening to children

Roxanne is playing at the dough table. Joanne, a childcare student, walks by. 'What is that you are making?' she asks Roxanne, looking down at her. 'Well, it is sort of a kind of small, squishy sort of thing…like a…', Roxanne replies. 'That's nice,' says Joanne quickly as she walks off.

▷ What was wrong with this conversation?

• • • *The importance of nursery rhymes, books and stories*

Children enjoy simple rhymes and action songs. If you watch a mother playing 'round and round the garden' with her baby, you can see the baby getting excited at the prospect of being tickled. By the time children are 4 years old, the rhyming sounds help them learn the sounds of different letters and words. In this way, rhymes are an important part of learning to read.

GIVE IT A GO nursery rhymes

Make a booklet with a collection of some of your favourite children's rhymes. Illustrate it with drawings or pictures cut from magazines. Try and find as many different types of rhyme as you can. If you know a toddler or young child, share some of your rhymes with him or her.

Children need to be able to enjoy books and stories regularly. It is never too early to start reading to children. As children get older they use books to gain information about the world and all its different people.

Books and stories allow children to:

- extend their vocabulary
- be entertained
- relax
- develop their imagination
- be comforted
- get information about things they may not experience directly.

We have already discussed the importance of respecting different cultures within our multicultural society. One of the most effective ways of doing this is through showing positive images of different people in different environments.

GIVE IT A GO positive images in books

Visit your local library and choose five different children's books.

1 Find out:

▢ if the books have pictures of people with different skin tones or names from a range of cultures

▢ if the text (writing) is all in English.

2 Now decide if the books you have chosen provide positive images of different cultures.

What children need

Security and safety

Because young babies are completely dependent on their adult carers, adults need to keep them safe and help them to feel secure. Babies need a familiar adult, a familiar environment, and to have their needs met. In order to meet a child's needs, you must find out as much as you can about the child:

- what he or she likes and dislikes
- what and when he or she eats
- when he or she needs a sleep
- what his or her favourite toys or comforters are.

CASE STUDY safety and security

Baby Charlene has been left with a neighbour called Sarah while her mum goes shopping. Charlene would not stop crying so Sarah put her in the pram and eventually she fell asleep exhausted. When she woke up, Sarah sat her in the corner of the sofa to give her some dinner. Sarah had prepared a shepherds pie but Charlene did not look happy when she tasted the mince, spat it out and started crying again. Sarah went to the kitchen to fetch Charlene a drink when she heard a loud thump. She rushed back into the living room to find that Charlene had fallen off the sofa and was lying on the floor very still.

▢ Why is Charlene not happy?

▢ What would have helped Charlene to feel safe and secure?

● ● ● *The importance of appropriate physical contact and touch*

Physical contact is the way of passing messages to a baby that he or she is loved and cared for. Very young babies recognise the voice and smell of their mother and feel safe and secure when being held.

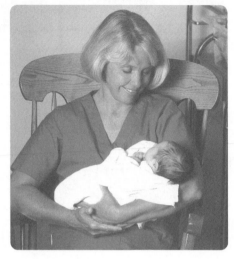

When holding a baby, you should:

- be confident
- hold him or her gently but firmly, close to your body
- support the head
- let him or her play with your fingers, hair and face
- stroke the baby gently.

How to hold a baby.

● ● ● *Why babies and young children cry*

There are many reasons why babies and young children cry.

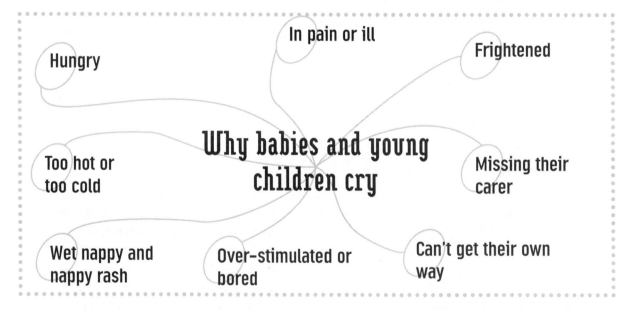

Hungry

In pain or ill

Frightened

Too hot or too cold

Why babies and young children cry

Missing their carer

Wet nappy and nappy rash

Over-stimulated or bored

Can't get their own way

● ● ● *How babies and young children can be comforted and distracted*

You need to find out the reason why the baby is crying. You could offer him or her a drink, check the baby's temperature or change his or her nappy. It is easier to identify why young children cry as they can often tell you.

To comfort a baby you can:

- cuddle him or her
- stroke the baby gently
- talk quietly to the baby
- sing to the baby
- distract him or her with stories
- distract him or her with other activities.

CASE STUDY) comforting children

It is Tom's first day at nursery. When his mum leaves he starts to cry. He stands at the door banging it and howling. An early years nurse picks him up and carries him to a comfy chair in the book corner where she holds him gently and talks quietly to him, telling him that mummy will be back soon. She acknowledges his fears by saying, 'You are very sad that mummy has gone shopping, but she will soon come back.' Then she picks up a book and quietly starts reading the story. Soon Tom stops crying. The early years nurse then gets him a drink of water and sits at the playdough table encouraging Tom to feel the dough. Tom is soon engrossed in his play and very happy making lots of long wiggly worms.

D What has the early years nurse done to help Tom stop crying?

Love and affection

Love and affection are essential for healthy emotional development. They help children to feel confident and secure in themselves and express their feelings.

● ● ● *How babies demonstrate affection*

Very young babies often stop crying when they are picked up. This is because they like physical contact and rely on an adult to make them feel comfortable. This is the early stage of growing affection. By the age of 6 weeks, the baby will begin to smile and respond to attempts at communication. He or she will show pleasure on seeing a familiar face by smiling, laughing or chuckling. The baby will hold out his or her arms to be picked up and cuddled.

● ● ● *Attachment and distress*

Young babies are able to feel secure by developing strong bonds with a few well-known carers. This bond is often called an 'attachment'. A baby develops a secure bond or attachment with the people who meet his or her needs, i.e. the people who pick the baby up when he or she cries, feed the baby and provide love and affection. The ability to make secure attachments is important to emotional development and helps the child to make good relationships later in life.

Around the age of 7–9 months, babies develop what is know as 'separation anxiety'. This means that they begin to show a fear of strangers and are unhappy if the adults that they know are out of sight. Babies will become distressed, cry and look around for a familiar adult.

CASE STUDY attachment and distress

Nadiah and Leonna have both got new jobs and have found childminders for their 8-month-old babies. Leonna had been on holiday so her baby had only met the childminder once before she was left alone with her. Nadiah had visited her childminder's house five or six times with her baby before she left her baby alone with the childminder.

▷ Which baby is likely to be most distressed when left with the new childminder?

▷ How will the baby show distress?

Social and emotional needs are met through providing a safe and secure environment:

Love and affection

Care from familiar adults

To feel good about themselves

Meeting social and emotional needs

Praise and encouragement

To have their needs met and know that someone will care for them

To feel safe and protected from harm

• • • *Effects on an infant of a lack of affection*

Without love and affection a child's emotional needs will not be met. This will affect all other areas of the child's development and result in a 'failure to thrive'. This is the term used when a child's development in all areas is delayed.

Failure to thrive:

- physical development – the child may be thin and often ill
- social development – the child may become withdrawn and reluctant to mix with others
- emotional development – the child may be unusually fearful or develop very challenging behaviour or habits such as head banging
- intellectual development – the child's ability to learn may be limited.

Patience and understanding

You have seen that children need a lot care and attention from adults to support their growth and development. Looking after babies and young children is not easy. You have to be able to understand their needs and then meet these needs. This often requires a lot of patience because you have to put their needs before your own.

WHAT if

Patience and understanding

...You were travelling on a train with a 4-year-old and a 2-year-old?

You are tired and have a headache. You want to read a magazine and then have a little sleep. Unfortunately, the children are very excited and are chatting and laughing. They get rather silly, so you tell them off. The older child starts to cry. 'I want a drink,' the younger child calls. You give them both a packet of juice and go back to your magazine. However, the children keep interrupting you and asking questions, and your headache is getting worse. Then, the younger child says that he needs to go to the toilet.

- What do these children need?
- Why is it difficult for you to meet their needs?
- What are you going to do?

● ● ● How attention and memory skills affect behaviour

Young children have a short attention span and find it difficult to concentrate on things for very long. This may be quite frustrating for an adult who wants to have a bit of peace and quiet while the children play. Children's memory skills have not developed fully, so when you tell a child not to do something, he or she will probably have forgotten by the next day – so repeat it!

| CASE STUDY | attention and memory |

Jenna is sitting on the floor looking happy, having pulled all the books off the bottom shelf of the bookcase. Her mother is very cross and says, 'For goodness sake, I gave you a jigsaw to play with only half and hour ago and I told you yesterday not to touch the books. Why won't you do what you are told?'

▷ Why has Jenna pulled the books from the shelf?

• • • *Understanding the world from a child's perspective*

What do we mean by 'good behaviour'? Do we actually mean doing what an adult tells a child to do? Do you always like doing what you are told? Of course not! Similarly, it is not easy for a child to 'behave'. Even if there are set rules, a young child may not understand the rules or may forget what the rules are. Sometimes the rules are different every day and this makes it very difficult for a child to know what is expected of him or her. It is particularly difficult if an adult shouts at a child, or tells him or her that he or she is naughty or stupid. This often frightens children and makes them feel very bad about themselves. The young child may not even understand what he or she has done wrong and this can be very confusing.

| CASE STUDY | mixed messages about how to behave |

Donna's mum says she cannot have a sweet after dinner, but Granny gives her one. Mum says Donna has to go to bed at 7 o'clock, but dad and the babysitter let her stay up till 9 o'clock. Donna has also learnt that when she is not allowed to do something, if she makes enough fuss, her mum relents and lets her have her own way. This is very muddling for Donna, who does not know what is expected of her. In fact, the only way that Donna's mum can make her behave is to shout at her very loudly.

▷ Why is it difficult for Donna to behave?

▷ Why is it important not to shout at Donna?

• • • *How to reinforce positive behaviour and discourage unwanted behaviour*

Children can be helped to behave appropriately (well) by having some simple rules that they understand, lots of praise when they behave appropriately and a good role model to copy.

To discourage a child's unwanted behaviour you should:

- Distract the child.
- Remind the child quietly what the rules are.
- Explain why the child should behave in the way that you want.
- Never say, 'You are a very bad child, I hate you.'
- Always say, 'I do not like what you did.' This lets the child know that you still love him or her although you do not approve of his or her behaviour.
- Never smack or shake a young child. It will not teach him or her how to behave, but will just show that it is alright to hit other people.

Managing behaviour

...*You were asked to deal with a child's unwanted behaviour?*

You are looking after two 4-year-old boys. They are sat in the back of the car that you are driving. They start to pinch each other and pull each other's hair.

▷ How do your respond to this unwanted behaviour?

●●● EVIDENCE ACTIVITY

Managing behaviour

Create a leaflet that could be given to parents to help them manage their child's behaviour. It should include:

▷ why it is difficult for children to behave

▷ ideas to help them manage their child's behaviour

▷ reasons why smacking is not good for children.

How to keep children physically healthy

Sleep and rest

Exercise

Good food

To keep healthy, children need:

Good hygiene routines

Care when they are ill

Exercise

All people should exercise regularly. In particular, children need exercise to promote growth and development. Exercise:

- strengthens bones and muscles
- improves coordination
- improves the circulation (the blood travelling round the body)
- makes the heart muscles work
- improves the appetite
- relieves stress and encourages good sleep patterns
- improves health in later life.

There are many ways to encourage children to be more active.

Exercise indoors	Exercise outdoors (with the advantage of fresh air)
Music and movement activities. Hopping, skipping and jumping. Dancing. Ring games, such as 'Here we go round the mulberry bush'.	'Sit and rides' and bikes. Climbing frames. Races. Team games. Walks in the park.

GIVE IT A GO   obstacle course

You have been asked to design an obstacle course for a group of 4-year-old children. You have been given a bench, a mat, a small climbing frame with a slide, a tunnel, five traffic cones and a piece of chalk to draw on the ground with. You should include opportunities for the children to run, jump, climb, hop and crawl. Draw your design on a piece of paper.

• • • *The importance of developing good exercise routines*

These days young children do not take enough exercise. This may increase the possibility of heart disease and poor health in later life. Many children are driven to school and spend much of their leisure time in front of the television. Children learn habits for life during early childhood. A person who eats well and takes regular exercise when young is likely to continue to eat well and take regular exercise as he or she grows older.

Sleep and rest

There are many reasons why sleep and rest are important:

- growth hormones work while asleep
- the body fights infection while asleep
- sleep provides energy for exercise
- sleep improves concentration
- sleep allows the body to relax.

• • • *Sleep patterns in infancy and childhood*

All children need different amounts of sleep. The table below describes the average sleep patterns for babies and young children.

New born baby	16–18 hours a day
9-month-old	14 hours a day; baby may take two naps during the day
2-year-old	12–14 hours; baby may take one nap during the day
4-year-old	12 hours; child will need a rest period during the day
8-year-old	9 hours

• • • *Encouraging good sleeping habits*

Your 'body clock' tells you when to get up and when to go to bed. In the same way, babies need to have a regular sleep routine otherwise they can become bad tempered and unhappy.

A sleep routine for a baby should include the following:

- the baby should be fed and have a nappy change
- the baby should sleep in a quiet place with dimmed lights and good ventilation
- the baby should be calmly and gently placed in the cot
- the adult may sing or talk quietly for a short time.

Older children should also have a regular bedtime routine, which may include bathing, teeth cleaning and a story.

WHAT if Sleep patterns

...you have to ensure three children get enough sleep?

You are looking after three children from 7.30 a.m. until 6.30 p.m.. Tommy is 9 months old, Tara is 2 years old and Tamsin is 4 years old. Make a chart for the day to show when each child will sleep.

Good food

Children need a balanced diet in order to:

- support growth
- make strong bones and healthy teeth
- keep healthy
- provide good eating habits for life.

• • • *The importance of breastfeeding*

Breastfeeding is important for physical health and neurological development.

Everyone agrees that breast milk is the best and healthiest first food for babies. There is growing evidence to show that babies who are artificially fed (i.e. with formula milk) are more at risk of some serious health consequences. For example, for babies whose families have a history of asthma, eczema or hay fever, breastfeeding reduces the likelihood of these conditions occurring by up to 50 per cent. Similarly, research has shown that babies who were breastfed are less likely to suffer from diseases such as coronary heart disease, obesity or diabetes in later life.

It is therefore very important that people know and understand the advantages and disadvantages of the different methods of feeding their babies. The way in which artificial milk has been marketed and promoted in the past has suggested that it is comparable to breast milk; however, current advertising regulations place strict controls on the claims that can be made for infant formula.

Helps the emotional bond to develop between mother and baby

Has all the nutrients the baby needs

Is cheaper than bottle feeding (it costs around £350 per year to use formula milk)

Breastfeeding

The milk is the correct temperature

Breast milk protects the baby from infection

Is more convenient than bottle feeding: no need to sterilise bottles and teats

Today, the government recommends, in line with the findings of the World Health Organisation, that mothers breastfeed their babies exclusively (that is, do not give any other food or drinks) for six months. Maternity and neonatal units have been advised to help mothers breastfeed by introducing policies based on the 'Ten steps to successful breastfeeding', developed by the World Health Organisation (see below).

Ten steps to successful breastfeeding:

1 Have a written breastfeeding policy that is routinely communicated to all healthcare staff.

2 Train all healthcare staff in the skills necessary to implement this policy.

3 Inform all pregnant women about the benefits and management of breastfeeding.

4 Help mothers to start breastfeeding within half an hour of birth.

5 Show mothers how to breastfeed and keep up their milk supply, even if they are separated from their infants.

6 Give newborn infants no food or drink other than breast milk (if possible).

7 While in hospital, allow mothers and infants to remain together 24 hours a day.

8 Encourage breastfeeding on demand (i.e. whenever the baby is hungry).

9 Do not give dummies to infants who are breastfeeding.

10 Encourage the establishment of breastfeeding support groups and refer mothers to them when they are discharged from hospital.

Difficulties with breastfeeding, for example, because a mother has to return to work, can be overcome if women learn how to express their breast milk so that it can be frozen and given in a bottle at a later time (following the instructions of bottle feeding – see page 209). A good time to express breast milk is first thing in the morning, before the first feed, when the breasts are full. After expressing, if the baby needs to feed, sucking will soon encourage more milk to flow.

Milk can be expressed by hand into a clean container or using a simple suction pump (bought at most chemists). A warm, clean facecloth placed over the breast will encourage milk to flow. The expressed milk can then be frozen in a sterilized ice-cube tray, placed in a bag. The cubes are then transferred to a storage bag and used as required. Just as mothers need to learn the skill of expressing milk, babies need to learn how to suck from a teat, because the technique is different.

GIVE IT A GO finding out about breastfeeding

Using the Internet, research the following organisations or resources that provide support for breastfeeding mothers:

▷ La Leche League – www.laleche.org.uk.

▷ National Childbirth Trust – www.nct-online.org

▷ Jane's Breastfeeding Resources – www.breastfeeding.co.uk

Note down your findings and then report them to the class.

• • • Appropriate alternatives to breastfeeding

There are many reasons why parents choose to feed their baby with infant formula; it is important that parents' wishes are respected and they are assisted with their chosen method of infant feeding. Formula milk comes as a powder which is mixed with boiled water. There are different types of formula milk; however, most infant formula is made from modified cows milk. Some babies are allergic to cows milk and must be fed a formula of soya milk, prescribed by a doctor. Babies under 6 months of age should not be given ordinary cows milk and should not start on solid food until they are at least 17 weeks of age.

• • • Bottle feeding safely

Young babies do not have much resistance to infection, so good hygiene procedures are very important when bottle feeding. Detailed guidelines for bottle feeding are given on the next page.

Guidelines for bottle feeding

Preparing the bottle:

- All equipment must be sterilised correctly following the instructions on the sterilising kit.
- Wash your hands.
- Gather all materials: the milk formula, a spoon, boiled water, sterilised feeding bottle and teat, and teat protector.
- Always use the correct amount of powder – too much or too little will harm the child.
- Mix well to ensure that the powder is properly dissolved.
- Cover the teat with the teat protector.
- Store the bottle in the fridge until ready for use.

Feeding the baby:

- Wash your hands.
- Warm the bottle in a jug of hot water or bottle warmer. Do not use a microwave.
- Check the temperature before giving the bottle to the child.
- Hold the baby gently in the crook of your arm.
- Tilt the bottle and ensure that the teat is always full of milk.
- Talk to the baby while feeding.
- Sit the baby up occasionally during the feed to allow the baby to release trapped wind.
- Never leave a baby alone with a bottle.

CASE STUDY · bottle feeding

Shelley came home late and was too tired to make the baby's bottle for the next day. At 4 a.m. the baby started crying. 'For goodness sake, get that baby a bottle and then we can go back to sleep,' Shelley's partner said. Shelley went down to the kitchen, put the kettle on and grabbed a bottle from the pile of washing-up beside the sink. She found the formula but couldn't find the measuring spoon, so she just scooped a few teaspoons into the bottle before adding the boiled water. The baby was still screaming, so she topped the bottle up with cold water to cool it quickly. Shelley then fed the baby and the crying stopped immediately. She propped the bottle up with a pillow so the baby could reach the teat, went back to bed and fell asleep.

▷ Find four things that Shelley has done wrong.

▷ What might happen to the baby as a result of this?

• • • *Weaning and feeding*

Weaning is when the baby starts to eat solid food. This happens at about 4–6 months of age. Solid foods are introduced slowly over a period of time. This allows you to detect if the baby is allergic to any new food.

Age	Type of food	Examples
4–6 months	Pureed food, quite runny and mixed with formula or breast milk.	Rice, vegetables and fruit.
6–9 months	Move towards mashed or minced food.	Meat, fish and well-cooked eggs can be introduced; wheat products at a later date.
9–12 months	Finger food. Babies should be encouraged to feed themselves with food they can hold, such as toast or bananas.	Cow's milk can be introduced. Babies can eat the same food as the family, so long as it is well mashed up.

Weaning – some key points:

- Exclusive breastfeeding is continued wherever possible for the first six months, as this will meet all the infants' requirements, including iron.
- Whether breast or bottle feeding, weaning does not begin until the infant has reached at least 17 weeks of age (4 months).
- Food other than milk should be introduced very slowly so that it does not make up a significant part of the diet.
- Breast or formula milk should be continued until at least 1 year of age.
- By the age of 1 year, the infant should be eating a wide range of foods.

• • • *Diets for young children*

Young children need a healthy and balanced diet which should include:

- proteins – e.g. meat, fish, eggs, soya, beans, lentils – for growth
- carbohydrates – e.g. cereals, bread, rice, pasta – to provide energy
- vitamins and fibre – e.g. vegetables and fruit – for good health and to prevent illness
- dairy products – e.g. milk, cheese, yoghurt – to provide calcium for strong bones and teeth
- fats and oils – e.g. butter, margarine, oils – but in small amounts only.

• • • *Drinks*

It has been identified that regular drinks of water help a child's intellectual development. Many schools now encourage children to drink water regularly during the day. Water and milk are healthy for children to drink. Avoid giving children drinks with a high sugar content, such as fizzy pop and fruit squash.

● ● ● *Good hygiene routines*

Babies and young children have not built up a resistance to infection, so good hygiene procedures are essential to reduce the possibility of infection.

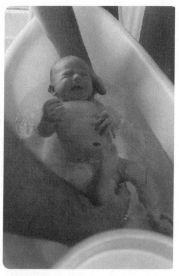
Bathing a baby.

It is important to keep children's skin, hair and teeth clean. However, you should always talk to the parents about any aspect of their child's care, for example, the type of shampoo they want you to use. Some families may use oil and plait their child's hair. Many toddlers and young children do not like having their hair washed, so you may need to use goggles or a protector to keep the water out of their eyes.

Very young babies may not require a bath every day, but their faces, hands and nappy area should be cleaned regularly throughout the day. Older children are often bathed every day as part of a bedtime routine.

Guidelines for bathing a baby

Do:
Prepare all the equipment.
Check the water temperature.
Be very gentle and support the baby's head.
Dry the baby very carefully.

Don't:
Wear a watch or jewellery.
Leave babies or children alone in or near water.
Allow the baby to become cold.

A baby's first tooth usually appears at about 6 months of age and cleaning should start at once.

Clean after food and at least twice a day

Avoid eating between meals

Limit the amount of sugary foods

Care of a child's teeth

Bottles should only be used for milk or water

Visit the dentist regularly

• • • *Toilet training*

The term 'toilet training' implies that an adult can 'train' a child to become dry. This is not true because children cannot control the bladder and bowel until they are able to:

- recognise that they need to use a potty
- ask an adult for the potty
- wait till the potty arrives.

This ability may develop as early as 15 months of age or it may not happen till the child is nearly 3 years old. The average age is about 2 years 4 months.

To help a child learn to use a potty, you should:

- have clothes that are easy for the child to take off
- have a potty that is easy to get to
- praise the child when he or she uses the potty
- don't get cross if the child has an accident.

⬤⬤⬤ EVIDENCE ACTIVITY

Daily routine

Return to the daily plan you made about children's sleep patterns (on page 206). Choose one of the children and describe a daily routine for that child that includes:

▢ sleep and rest periods   ▢ opportunities for exercise

▢ meals   ▢ washing and bathing opportunities.

• • • *Care during illness*

Most childcare settings encourage parents to keep their child at home if he or she is ill. However, your role is to recognise when a child is ill. Signs of illness include:

- the child has a fever, is hot and sweating or cold and clammy
- a pale or flushed appearance
- vomiting or diarrhoea
- the appearance of a rash or spots
- pain (children often cannot describe where a pain is, so unexplained crying may be a sign of pain)
- a change in behaviour, e.g. the child becomes irritable or withdrawn
- falling asleep at unusual times.

• • • *When to call a doctor*

A doctor should be called if:

- the child cannot drink anything without vomiting
- the child appears dehydrated (e.g. headache, dark urine, dry skin and mouth, a pale colour)
- there is a very high temperature
- there is a rash that does not disappear when pressed with a glass
- you are worried about any of the signs described above.

• • • *Routine health checks*

Throughout childhood, children have regular routine health checks to ensure that they are developing normally. The child will be measured and weighed, have hearing tests or eye tests, and his or her language development will be checked. These checks are usually carried out at:

- birth
- 6–8 weeks
- 6–9 months
- 18–24 months
- 3–3½ years
- when staring school.

• • • *Immunisations*

As well as the regular health checks, babies and young children are offered an immunisation programme. This means giving the child an injection which prevents the child developing serious illnesses. Some of the diseases that can be prevented are:

- Tuberculosis (TB)
- Diphtheria
- Whooping cough
- Measles
- Mumps and German measles
- Polio.

Some babies may have a mild reaction and feel a little ill following a vaccination. Some parents choose not to have their child vaccinated.

⬤⬤⬤ EVIDENCE ACTIVITY

Children's health

1 Visit a doctor's surgery and collect a range of leaflets about children's health. Make a display to share with your class, to develop your understanding of children's health.

2 Make a poster that you could display on the wall of a health centre where parents take their babies for routine health checks. The poster should describe all the things parents should do to keep their babies healthy.

unit 8

Images of people

In this unit you will explore the way our society views and treats different groups of people, and the impact this can have on their health and well-being.

You will explore stereotypical images (thinking about people or groups of people as being 'all the same type') for a range of different population groups and look for ways to make sure that you do not hold stereotypical views. You will also look at ways of challenging the stereotypical views of others.

Finally, you will examine issues relating to discrimination. A good explanation of discrimination is 'treating people differently because of their race, religion, ethnicity, age or gender (sex)'. Discrimination could also be as a result of some other 'difference', for example, sexual orientation.

In this unit you will learn about:

- society's images of different groups of people
- discrimination and its effects on individuals
- how to avoid discriminatory practice
- the benefits to individuals of avoiding discriminatory practice.

Before you start

GIVE IT A GO   reasons for discrimination

What reasons might cause a person to discriminate against others?

Some key words used in this unit are:

- **stereotype** – a fixed image or way of thinking about a group of people, which is usually incorrect.
- **images** – the way we see individuals and groups of people, for example, the image you see when you think of 'cowboys' in American films is likely to be a 'stereotype'.
- **society** – the term used when referring to many people living and working in the same area; this could be a ward, town, region or country.
- **discrimination** – treating people or groups of people less well than others because they differ from you.

Images of different groups of people

All groups of people have images associated with them. Sometimes these images are written down and sometimes they are the thoughts and feelings that other people have about others. Images can be very helpful when we are trying to explain something to others.

You have already tried to think of an image when you were asked about 'cowboys' in an American film. What image did you come up with? Perhaps you saw a man riding on a horse, wearing a gunbelt and hat. Perhaps you even visualised him riding through the desert.

GIVE IT A GO   images of groups of people

For each group write down three key words that you would use to describe these people to others:

▢ teenagers   ▢ toddlers   ▢ older people.

Now compare your three words for each age group with those of someone else from your group. Are there any words that are the same or nearly the same?

When writing down key words for 'toddlers', you may have written 'noisy', 'exhausting' and 'funny'. It is when we all hold the same vision about a group of people that we can say they share the same image.

In the main, holding an image about a group of people can be helpful, but this is not the case if the image becomes negative and actually affects how a person or group of people are treated by others.

In this unit, you will be exploring images around different groups of the population:

- religious groups
- older people
- males and females
- ethnic groups
- people with disabilities.

Religious groups

Most people belong to some kind of religious group, and often this is a formal religion that has many rules and responsibilities. In the UK today there are many different formal religions. They share a common belief in an 'afterlife' – a place to go to once you die, and most hold a supreme being at the centre of their beliefs.

GIVE IT A GO   religions

How many religions can you think of in one minute? Ask someone to time the minute while you write a list of the religions that you know.

Some of the more common religions are:

- Sikhism
- Islam
- Judaism
- Christianity – both Roman Catholicism and Church of England.
- Buddism
- Rastafarianism
- Hinduism

GIVE IT A GO   investigating a religion

Working with another student, choose one of the religions listed above (or another if you prefer) and find out as much as you can about that religion. Make a wall poster that explains your findings to other people in your group.

In addition to formal religions, many people follow less formal religious beliefs. For such people, religion is often more about spirituality and being 'at one with the universe.' These people may believe in a supreme creator that is different to those in formal religions, and that life after death also occurs in a different form.

Some people hold no religious beliefs at all. They feel that once this life is over, everything is finished and the only way people 'go on' is through their children and grandchildren.

Religious differences

...You or your family hold religious or spiritual beliefs?

How do you think these are seen by others? How do you see them? Do you think that there is a difference in perception?

Older people

The term 'older people' is an interesting one. What does it mean to you?

GIVE IT A GO images of older people

Before reading further, ask your colleagues what they mean by 'older person.' Make notes of what they tell you.

The term 'older person' means different things to different people. When you are 16 years old, an older person could be anyone over the age of 30! When you are 30 years old, it could be anyone over the age of 50, and so on.

CASE STUDY who is the older person?

Miriam has just taken up writing short stories and poems for children. She has always been interested in writing. Now that she has time on her hands, she has decided to go to evening classes to learn how to write.

Learning to fly has always been an ambition for Uzma. Someone has just given her five free flying lessons for her 'special birthday' present. The instructor is a bit worried about taking someone with arthritis flying, but Uzma's doctor has said that it will not be a problem.

Fred is learning to map read and survive on the hills. He thinks walking and camping is boring but he does not want to hurt his father's feelings. His father has always walked the hills and hopes that one day his son will be out there with him.

Who would you say is the oldest person in the case study? Why have you made that decision? Discuss your findings with another person to see if they agree with you or if there are any differences in your thinking.

In health, social care and early years, an older person might be someone who has retired from work or someone who is fragile and vulnerable and needs help with his or her care needs. The government sees older people as those who are entitled to draw their 'old age pension'.

It is important to recognise that older people are no different to the rest of society. They may be living in a house on their own, or they might be married or sharing a house with a partner. They might have physical disabilities or learning difficulties. They might need additional support with their everyday living needs or they might not. We should be able to see that the term 'older people' means different things for everyone. Just like religion, there is no one definition that serves to explain what we mean by the term 'older people'.

Males and females

It should be easy to hold an image of male or female. But is it? When we talk about male and female, we are often talking about behaviour traits, i.e. the actions, behaviours, thoughts and feelings often associated with being a male or a female.

GIVE IT A GO the 'male' image

What image do you use to describe a male? Compare your image with another person. Are there any differences?

Males were traditionally associated with being strong, earning the income for the home and doing very little housework. Females, on the other hand, were traditionally seen as the carers in the home. If they did go out to work their income was seen as secondary to the man's income. Are these images a true reflection of today's society?

Today, most women go out to work and often earn more than their partners do. More men are staying at home as 'house husbands'. Society is changing and we no longer hold the same images of male and female that were held, for example, fifty years ago.

Ethnic groups

This is another 'group' of the population that is difficult to describe. There are many different ethnic groups but they all have 'things' in common. People who share the same ethnic group share the same 'gene pool', i.e. they share the same ancestors. This often means that people in the same ethnic group have similar physical characteristics. For example, people from Sweden and Denmark are often known for being very tall and having very blonde hair.

GIVE IT A GO ethnic groups

Which ethnic group do you belong to?

People with disabilities

People with a disability may feel very differently about their disability compared to others who do not share it.

CASE STUDY wheelchair athlete

Bronwen is a wheelchair user who recently attended school for the first time. She looks forward to going every day. When she plays basketball with the other children she can tell they 'feel sorry' for her because she cannot run alongside them. She wonders if she should tell them that she wants them 'to get a move on' and get out from under her wheels, as they get in her way during the game.

The term 'disabilities' is often used with a wide range of meanings in mind. We need to know that there are different disabilities and that we should not 'lump' people with disabilities together. These include:

- physical disabilities
- mental disabilities (learning difficulties)
- sensory disabilities.

These are considered in greater detail later in this unit (pages 229–230).

⬛⬛⬛ EVIDENCE ACTIVITY

Stereotypical images

Collect a range of images (pictures) of older people and teenagers from books, magazines, journals and leaflets, and make a poster out of them.

Use the poster to tell other people how the pictures compare to stereotypical images commonly associated with older people and teenagers. Include an explanation of how the images shown are *relevant* to stereotyping.

Suggest to others how the pictures could be changed to present a non-stereotypical image of that group, and explain the benefits of this to older people and teenagers, and to society in general.

Negative images

When we talk about 'negative images', we mean applying a picture or description to a group of people that is usually untrue and unjust. When we use a negative image in our thinking and our work, we may find that we treat people unfairly as a result. In our work and in all aspects of our lives, this should never happen. All people are entitled to be treated equally and fairly.

When we talk about negative images we are often referring to:

- stereotypical images
- assumptions
- labelling
- gender bias.

• • • *Stereotypical images*

There are many groups in the population that have had stereotypical images associated with them. These are used in books and newspapers, on the television and in films, or in other places, and they reinforce stereotypical views.

How do these pictures reflect stereotypical images of a tramp (left) and a monk (right)?

GIVE IT A GO stereotypical images

1 Have you ever noticed that the road traffic sign for 'older people' shows two bent people using walking sticks? This stereotypical image suggests that all older people will end up bent over and having to use a walking stick! Is this really the case?

2 Can you think of any other stereotypical images? Explore some magazines and books (especially older books if you can get them) to see what kind of images are often associated with some groups of the population. Look at newspaper reports about crimes to see if you can find stereotypical images.

• • • *Assumptions*

Making assumptions is similar to holding stereotypical images. When we make an assumption we are deciding what a person or group of people will be like before making the effort to find out for ourselves. To make assumptions we use information that we have previously collected (usually from a variety of sources) to guess what people are like. For example, making an assumption that you will not like someone before you meet that person because he or she had an argument with your friend. Another way of making an assumption is expecting people to eat or do certain things because of some aspect of their life. For example, we know that many religions forbid followers to eat meat; however, this does not mean that everyone of that religion will follow the rules.

CASE STUDY a wrong assumption

Monica has a penfriend that she has been in contact with for over a year. She has never met her before but she knows that she is a Muslim girl from a very traditional and religious family. She is meeting her for the first time at the railway station. When Shanaz arrives, Monica is surprised by her appearance. She is wearing jeans, ankle boots and a very stylish top with a long, knotted scarf thrown carelessly over her shoulders. 'Wow!' thought Monica, 'she looks terrific, not at all what I expected!'

▷ What assumptions do you think Monica had made about her pen friend?

▷ What assumptions do you hold about people from a traditional Muslim background?

• • • *Labelling*

Labelling is the term used when another person gives an individual a stereotypical name. It is a form of discrimination because labelling is usually negative and means that the person who has been labelled is treated differently from others.

CASE STUDY negative labels

Serina has two small boys aged 2½ years and 16 months. She is finding the care of these children very difficult. She has asked her health visitor to try to organise respite care for the older of the two boys because he is very active and is tiring her out. She is worried that by asking for help her son will be labelled 'disruptive' or 'badly behaved'.

▷ How likely do you think it is that Serina's son will be labelled in this way? How might such a label affect him during his time at nursery or infant school?

Once a label has been applied to an individual, it is very hard to shake off. People often 'see' evidence of the behaviour even when it is not there. Serina's eldest son could easily be labelled as 'difficult' or something similar whilst he is in respite care. It is possible that he will hear this label as he gets older and will tailor his behaviour to prove to others that he is indeed 'difficult'.

• • • *Gender bias*

When we discussed images of male and female, we said that men and women are of different sexes. This means that there is a biological difference between them. However, when we talk about 'gender', we are referring to the roles that each of the sexes adopt.

People who are gender biased often hold stereotypical views about the roles and responsibilities of males and females. For example, they see men as having heavy, labouring jobs and being the head of the household. This is an old-fashioned view that is not acceptable in today's society.

CASE STUDY | gender bias

Tina is a qualified nursery nurse. She did her training 25 years ago and enjoys working with children. Today is dressing-up day for the children and Toby wants to put on his apron and do some baking in the kitchen. Tina tells him that he is being 'soft' and would have a much better time playing at being a doctor.

D How is Tina demonstrating gender bias? What might be the results of this kind of attitude and approach to boys and girls? What would you do differently?

Positive images

It is important in care work of any kind to present a positive image of all groups and individuals. We should never be involved in presenting or promoting negative images. The damage that can arise from the resulting negative actions and behaviours to those groups and individuals can be devastating. Presenting positive images is all to do with what we say, how we say it and how we show it.

• • • *Non-stereotypical images*

We present a non-stereotypical image when we show respect for people as individuals, i.e. when we recognise that everyone is different and will want to do things that are different from each other. People will be interested in a whole range of activities and they will have different likes and dislikes depending on who they are. In other words, we should not stereotype people together but respect and value their differences.

It is important for care workers to also realise that we should respect and value each other, and that we should not present negative, stereotypical images in our work.

Look back to the Case Study on page 217.

CASE STUDY | a non-stereotypical image

It is possible that you selected Mirium or Uzma as the eldest of the three people. In fact it was Fred! His father is 82 years old and still walks the hills regularly. Fred is 58 years old and has just retired from work, and to please his father has taken up the same hobby for the first time.

▷ Do you think this image of Fred and his father is non-stereotypical? Why?

CASE STUDY | challenging stereotypes

John has enjoyed nursing for over ten years. He is a fully qualified staff nurse working on a busy medical ward that treats people of all ages for a wide range of conditions. He has just been accepted into midwifery training school. He knows he will have a lot of challenges to face but he is looking forward to it.

▷ What challenges do you think John will face?

▷ What do you think expectant mothers will think about having a male midwife?

▷ What kind of nursing care do you think they will expect?

▷ Will that care be any different when provided by a male or a female midwife?

It is a fact, not a stereotype, that in health, social care and early years services, most of the staff involved in caring for others are women. However, if we always show care being provided by women then we do not offer men the chance to make a difference, and we are contributing to the stereotypical images being presented.

Positive role models

A positive role model is a situation or person that demonstrates good values, respects rights and values diversity. For example, famous models who are not 'stick thin' or a 'pop star' who actively promote the no-smoking message.

CASE STUDY   the anti-drug message

Milly is a singer. Her brother was recently injured in a road traffic accident after taking a dance drug. She knows he will never walk again. She has decided to write a song about the dangers of drug taking and is having it released in time for the summer holidays. In the meantime, she is visiting colleges and schools promoting the anti-drug message.

We learn from the people around us all the time. Very often we learn without even knowing that we are learning. This is why we need to spend time and effort thinking about what we are doing and the messages we give out to other people through our behaviour.

People who work in the caring services need to demonstrate that they are a positive role model for everybody they come across. What would you think about a doctor who was always found drunk in the local nightclub?

Bethany Hamilton lost her arm in a shark attack but continues to surf in competitions. She is a positive role model for many young people.

GIVE IT A GO   identifying role models

Fill in the chart to identify other role models that have had a big influence on your life.

The role model	What I learned	What I respected
Parent	How to behave in public, to have good manners, to work hard.	The time my mum spent with me showing me how to do different things.

CASE STUDY — not a good role model

Tanvi is an early years nursery owner with a small daughter. She was seen in the local supermarket last week by a member of her team, losing her temper with her little girl who had just thrown a tantrum. Tanvi became exasperated and finally slapped her daughter before sitting her down hard in the shopping trolley.

▷ What kind of a role model is Tanvi being for her member of staff and future clients?

• • • *Respecting diversity*

Respecting diversity is part of the care value base (see pages 63–65). It is an important part of working in health, social care and early years provision. If we cannot respect and value the differences between people, we will never be able to successfully appreciate the world around us.

So how do we demonstrate respect for diversity and difference? It is not always an easy thing to do but we can start by examining our expectations of other people.

GIVE IT A GO — examining our expectations

Think about your friends with different beliefs to your own. Do you have one who is vegetarian? Or do you have a friend who believes in only using products that have not been tested on animals? Maybe you have a belief that differs from those of your friends.

▷ How would you behave towards your friend(s) as a result of their beliefs?
▷ How do you expect them to behave towards you as a result of your beliefs?

CASE STUDY — showing respect

Re-read the story of Samina on page 65.

▷ Why does this example demonstrate respect?

The role of the media

When we talk about the media we mean:

- television
- newspapers
- magazines and books
- posters
- leaflets

- the Internet
- email
- CD-ROMs
- videos
- mobile phones and other electronic forms of communication.

• • • *Books*

Books have an important role to play in creating images that we learn to associate with. Sometimes these images are shown through pictures and sometimes the images are created through words.

A good book will always show a range of different images. For example, a children's story book should show children with a range of different skin tones. Books should show boys and girls becoming involved in a range of activities that are not stereotyped to one particular sex, and they should show the opportunities included as available to all the characters.

GIVE IT A GO | children's books

Select two children's books and have a look to see if they show evidence of promoting a positive image. Discuss with another student what it is that creates the positive (or negative) image.

• • • *Leaflets*

Leaflets are often used to provide health information or information to a parent about their child, so they need to be in a range of languages to enable the target audience to read and understand them.

• • • *Newspapers and magazines*

Newspapers have a very important role to play in presenting positive images, but sometimes the stories they carry have a stereotypical aspect and it can be difficult to challenge this. However, 'good' news stories often involve people from all walks of life who have achieved something special. This helps to show good role models for other people.

GIVE IT A GO | negative images in the press

Have a look through a range of newspapers to see if you can find evidence of negative labelling or stereotypical images and articles. Cut them out and make a poster to demonstrate how newspapers promote negative images.

Magazines and newspapers should be able to present positive images to their readers and not be stereotypical in their approach. They should include all population groups in their features and they need to ensure that these population groups are not shown in a negative way. Magazines and newspapers have a clear role and responsibility to promote good role models to their readers.

• • • *Television*

The media has a direct route into our homes and workplaces and because of this can influence both positive and negative images of people. For example, if older people are always shown to be forgetful and infirm on soap operas, then it is possible that a whole generation of viewers will grow up with a stereotypical view of older people.

GIVE IT A GO   researching television

Choose a television programme and a group of the population that you have already studied, and make notes about the way that population group is portrayed in the programme. Describe your findings to the rest of your group.

Your role

Individuals also have a role to play in creating positive images about different population groups.

GIVE IT A GO   what you can do

What can you do as an individual to ensure that positive images of different population groups are shown or discussed? Make notes of your thoughts.

Challenge your own ideas and thoughts if you think they might be stereotypical

Talk about men and women doing non-traditional jobs

Challenge negative comments when you hear them

You could …

Get to know as many different people as possible

Point out stereotypical images to others so that something can be done about them

Discrimination and its effects

In the main, discrimination is usually about treating a person differently (less well) for some reason. Whatever the reason, it is likely to have a negative effect on that person's health and well-being. All the forms of discrimination discussed in this section are illegal in the health, social care and early years sectors.

Ageism

Ageism is discrimination against a person because of his or her age. It is important to recognise that ageism is not only about older people.

CASE STUDY — ageism at work

Tahir is 19 years old and really wants to be an assessor in a nursing home for older people. He has worked as a carer for three years and has obtained his NVQ Level 3 in Care. He has been helping his manager to train new carers for the past twelve months and thinks he should be allowed to study for his assessor's qualification. At his last appraisal, his manager said that she thought he was too young and would not have the respect of care trainees who were much older than him, therefore despite his good work he should wait another five years.

▷ Discuss this example of ageism with another student. What do you think about the manager's point. Is she right? Should Tahir wait another five years?

It is more important that Tahir can demonstrate he can do the job that is required rather than be 'the right age'. He can gain respect in other ways; for example, by:

- being knowledgeable
- providing good guidance to trainees
- being fair and accurate in assessments made
- being supportive
- being a good role model.

Because ageism is no longer allowed by law, many job applications do not ask for a person's age and, when selecting candidates for interviews, name, age and sex are not shown in the details. This is so that the people who are shortlisting (asking someone to come for an interview) will not be influenced either negatively or positively by the personal information about the individuals.

Racism

The term 'race' refers to people who come from the same gene pool (as with ethnicity). In the UK today there are many different population groups.

GIVE IT A GO   web research

Log on to the Commission for Racial Equality (CRE) website – www.cre.gov.uk – to find out the latest information about racial issues.

In the health, social care and early years services, the needs of all people from all races are to be respected equally. As a healthcare worker it is your duty to see that each person's individual needs are met.

Sexism

Sexism is treating people differently because they are either a man or woman, or because of their sexual orientation. This means discriminating against people because they are, for example, homosexual or bisexual, or because of some other aspect of their sexual lives.

Disability discrimination

• • • *Physical disability*

Physical disability refers to any part of the human body that is not functioning fully. For example, if you have a pair of legs it is assumed you will be able to walk; however, there are a whole list of medical reasons, including accident or disease, that could prevent you from walking.

There are many aspects to physical disability that should be considered. For example, there are differing levels of disability and that person will have his or her own attitude towards the disability. We should therefore be guided by individual circumstances.

All shops and public buildings, including hospitals, nurseries and care homes, must ensure that they can provide their services to every individual no matter what their ability or disability. This means that an employer or service provider cannot use access (design of the building) as a reason for not employing someone with a disability.

GIVE IT A GO   respecting disability

Access www.disabilitygo.com to find out more about how shops, businesses and other services can meet the needs of those with disabilities.

• • • *Mental disability (learning difficulty)*

Mental illness can be caused by a variety of different issues, including disease and injury, but here we concentrate on learning difficulties. There are a wide range of learning difficulties, for example, dyslexia can be classed as a learning difficulty.

• • • *Sensory disability*

A sensory disability is one that involves one or more of the five senses – sight, hearing, touch, taste and smell. The most common sensory disabilities relate to sight and hearing. It is important that we find ways of enabling people to participate fully in the service we offer no matter what their disability. For example, people who cannot see may wish to use talking books or books written in Braille as an alternative to reading books and newspapers. People who are deaf may wish to use text telephones and text television. You need to know about these services so that you can enable your clients to access them.

A blind person reading Braille.

Types of discrimination

There are two main types of discrimination:

- discrimination at an individual level
- discrimination at an institutional level.

CASE STUDY | making assumptions

Steve is a carer who carries out home visits to people who need additional support with their everyday care needs. He has a new client on his list called Malcolm. According to his care plan, Malcolm is a follower of the Rastafarian religion. 'Oh no', thought Steve, 'he will be into taking drugs and is sure to have dreadlocks that have not been washed for weeks. I bet I will have to spend hours with him!'

▷ What assumptions is Steve making about Malcolm? Do you think his assumptions are likely to be true?

When Steve reaches Malcolm's home he finds several people all meeting to discuss the new youth club they are trying to open. Malcolm explains that they are hoping it will act as a safe place for young people to come to instead of being on the streets. He is keen to keep youngsters out of the drug scene. As for dreadlocks, the only outward sign of Malcolm's religion is the red, yellow and green hat that he is wearing. It turns out that Steve's assumptions were very wrong! Steve has learned a valuable lesson about not making assumptions about individuals.

• • • *Individual level discrimination*

At an individual level, discrimination is usually about the behaviour of one person to another or to a group of other people. It can be seen as negative and based upon assumptions and stereotypical attitudes. Very often our behaviour towards other people is based upon the information that we have learnt as a small child. Sometimes this information is wrong because of outdated attitudes or existing assumptions. Once we have grown up, however, we can make our own decisions about people.

CASE STUDY | discrimination in a nursery setting

Kat is an early years nursery nurse. She has been in her job for six months. She enjoys the work but knows she has to pay special attention and give more time to Rita who is from an Asian Heritage background. Kat is quite sure that if she does not spend time with her she will grow up to be 'backward'. 'Everyone knows that children from this culture never have any toys to play with, so they never get the chance to learn', she thinks. Kat feels very cross with the parents and so makes every effort not to speak to them.

▷ Discuss with another person the kind of discrimination that is happening here? What advice would you give to Kat if you worked alongside her?

In the above example, it is clear that Kat is not only making assumptions but she is also discriminating against Rita's parents. If you look carefully you can also see that she is discriminating against the other children as well: she should be dividing her attention equally across all the children.

CASE STUDY | deliberate discrimination

Mrs Patel is a dentist. She has a busy surgery with a wide range of different client groups. If there is one thing she cannot stand, it is single mothers who are out of work. Joy is in her surgery now with another bout of toothache. 'I bet she is claiming benefit again for her treatment. She is just too lazy to go and look for work. Well, she can just wait until the very end of surgery before I put myself out for her,' thinks Mrs Patel.

▷ What kind of discrimination is this? What do you think has influenced Mrs Patel's assumptions. Is she likely to be right?

• • • *Institutional level discrimination*

Sometimes discrimination is much harder to spot than the case studies above have shown. When we talk about discrimination at an institutional level, we are talking about discrimination that is built in to the way an organisation is run.

It has been said that the UK healthcare system is 'institutionally racist' and discriminates against people who are not white and middle class. To some extent this may be true. The health and social care service was set up in the mid-1940s when the population mix was very different. At that time, some groups of the population, for example, people who could not read and write, found it very difficult to get the service they were entitled to. Today, there are other difficulties that service users might have.

CASE STUDY | needing a female doctor

Shazia needs to go to the family planning clinic as she is getting married shortly and her husband agrees that they do not want to start a family for a couple of years. She has made an appointment to see the family planning doctor and is horrified to find out that it will be a male doctor. There is no way that Shazia will discuss such matters with a man. She asks to see a female doctor but is told there isn't one available, and that if she wants to use the service she will have to use what is provided.

How is this an example of institutional discrimination? What could be done differently?

Health, social care and early years services are changing very rapidly to ensure that everyone has equal access to them and is treated the same. All services have to have an equal opportunities policy.

Effects of discrimination

Discrimination can result in:

- physical injury
- isolation
- poor health
- fear

- low self-esteem
- lack of confidence
- depression
- poor work opportunities.

CASE STUDY | the effects of racism

Jamal attends his local college where he is studying to be an IT technician. He hates it at college because there are some guys in his class who are clearly racist. They are always making comments about his skin colour, the clothes he wears and the food he eats. This upsets him, however, the worst thing is that they have threatened to 'beat him up' if they ever catch him away from the college premises.

Jamal now spends all his time alone at home. He is depressed, fed up and worried about his personal safety. He just doesn't see how he can continue with his studies.

CASE STUDY   the effects of racism continued

▷ Look at the list of effects of discrimination on page 232 and choose the ones you think Jamal is suffering from? Make notes of your decisions, stating why and how the discrimination is affecting him.

If this situation is allowed to continue, Jamal will lose his confidence completely and his self-esteem (the way he feels about himself) will be affected. If our self-esteem is high we have confidence and can tackle anything, but when our self-esteem is low we are often unwilling to try anything new because we don't believe in ourselves.

GIVE IT A GO   forms of discrimination

Working with another person, use personal research (newspapers, the Internet or questioning people) to find out ways in which others have been discriminated against. Make a poster to show the effects of discrimination on these people.

⬤⬤⬤ EVIDENCE ACTIVITY

Discrimination

Make a display for people working in a care setting of your choice. The display should:

▷ Describe the forms of discrimination experienced by older people or teenagers (or another group if you prefer).

▷ List the effects of discrimination on physical, social and emotional well-being.

▷ Include two case studies showing the effects of discrimination on the physical, social or emotional well-being of your chosen group.

▷ Show how discrimination may affect the provision of care for your chosen group.

▷ List the benefits of avoiding discriminatory practice in the care setting.

▷ Show how stereotypical images and discrimination can be avoided in a carer's daily work practice.

Avoiding discriminatory practice

It is often up to the individuals concerned to make sure that they do not discriminate either deliberately or by accident (through ignorance). As health, social care and early years workers it is part of the code of ethics. We are expected to treat all people equally and fairly. We are also expected to respect diversity and value difference.

It is easy to avoid discriminatory practice with just a little thought. You have already seen in an earlier case study how a carer was able to help her client to pray at the times she needed to (see page 65). You can also avoid discriminatory practice in other ways.

Allowing clients to state a preference

This means giving your clients a choice. Never assume that clients want or need something just because you offer it and they are not in a position to get it themselves. Choices could include:

* choosing clothes to wear
* choosing a meal
* choosing to go out for entertainment
* choosing to watch certain television channels
* choosing music to listen to
* choosing to get involved with hobbies or activities.

Every client has the right to make choices and you should take care to offer them a choice at every opportunity.

CASE STUDY) choosing a meal

Simon is a home care worker and today he is cooking a meal for Albert and Doris who are both frail older people living in their own home. When he arrives, he has a look in the fridge to see what food is available. There is some fish, eggs and cheese.

▷ How could Simon offer a choice to his clients? What happens if they are too ill to make a choice or simply cannot be bothered? What would you do?

In any situation where you are dealing with people who are ill or unable to make a choice for some reason, care must be taken. The things you would need to take into account, for example, are the individual's:

* lifestyle
* religion
* culture

* race
* age
* ability.

Providing translation or interpretation facilities

This aspect of avoiding discriminatory practice is very important for service users who do not have English as a first language. At all opportunities you should ensure that written or spoken information is available in the first language of the individual. Sometimes this is just not possible, for example, many chemists (pharmacies) would not be able to provide medicine labels in any language other than English.

Interpreters – those who are fluent in several languages – are very useful in helping clients to understand a situation (e.g. a course of treatment). However, translation or interpretation is not always an easy option for the care services. This is because:

- there may not be anyone available who can translate or interpret the information
- the cost of using translation or interpretation services
- the time available for this
- the range of different languages required.

Despite these difficulties, every effort should be made to ensure that you do not discriminate by excluding someone from accessing the information that he or she needs.

CASE STUDY discriminatory practice

Mira has an appointment at the antenatal clinic to check that all is well with her pregnancy. She has brought her 12-year-old son with her because she does not speak English and she knows that the staff do not speak her language. Mira needs to have a scan and an examination, and is asked to remove her clothes in preparation. She looks totally embarrassed and so does her son.

▷ How does this situation discriminate against Mira? What could the service provider do to help Mira gain access to the information she needs?

Ensuring food choices meet religious requirements

Today, most hospitals offer a menu that a patient can use to show what food choices they would like. However, this is not always the case in other establishments.

GIVE IT A GO food choices on offer

Working with another student, find out what kind of food choices are offered in an early years centre and a day care centre for older people. You could perhaps telephone to collect this information.

CASE STUDY respecting religious requirements

Basil is staying in respite care for two weeks. He is really worried about his stay because he follows the Jewish religion and wants to have his food prepared and served in accordance with religious observances. He has already asked his key worker about the food arrangements but she has not given him any further information.

Why is this issue important to Basil? What should the key worker be doing to demonstrate positive practice?

Undertaking care procedures in a respectful and empathetic manner

• • • Empathy

Empathy means 'having the ability to put yourself in someone else's place'. In other words, to be able to know what it must feel like to be in their situation.

Sometimes study centres encourage their students to spend a few hours in a wheelchair to find out what it is like being a wheelchair user – this would encourage empathy. Imagine how you would feel if you needed someone to take you to the toilet and then carry out all the intimate tasks associated with this.

• • • Respect

When we care for individuals we need to remember to be:

- kind
- careful
- supportive
- non-judgemental.
- professional
- knowledgeable
- good at our work

Respect can be demonstrated in many ways.

CASE STUDY demonstrating respect

Lynda works in a care home for frail, older people who need additional support. In the morning she helps Nancy with her personal care. She knocks on the door to ask Nancy's permission to enter the room and says, 'Good morning, Nancy. Have you slept well?' She then asks Nancy what she would like to wear today and gets her clothes ready before offering Nancy the choice of a shower, wash or bath. On the way downstairs, she chats with Nancy about her breakfast choices and some of the activities that are planned for the day.

Discuss with another person how Lynda's behaviour demonstrates respect.

Institutional responsibilities

One of the ways of making sure an organisation is anti-discriminatory is by making sure it has relevant policies and procedures in place.

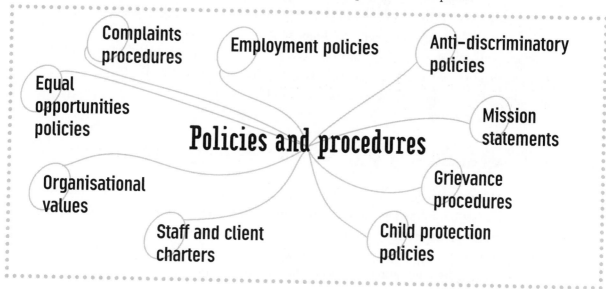

GIVE IT A GO   anti-discriminatory policies

1 Choose one of the anti-discriminatory policies described above to investigate further.

2 Working in a small group, make a wall display to show the range of policies and procedures that may be found in the health, social care and early years sectors.

Having these policies in place is not enough to ensure that anti-discriminatory practice does not take place. Someone has to make sure that the policies are working and kept up-to-date. In large organisations this is the job of the human resources department; in smaller services, managers and owners have the responsibility. In addition, external inspectors and internal staff monitor all policies and procedures. This is another way of making sure that the service is fulfilling its responsibilities to its clients.

Taking positive action

An organisation can demonstrate that it is avoiding discriminatory practice by taking positive action. For example, there will be occasions when an individual wants to make a complaint about some aspect of the service. He or she should be able to use the setting's policies and procedures to guide him or her.

CASE STUDY | making a complaint

Mary works as a member of a care team that looks after children with learning disabilities. She works full-time but does not earn enough money to keep her family as she is a single parent with two children. Sal, a member of Mary's team, found out that Mary claims benefits from her brother, who works for the Benefit Agency. Sal was caught telling other staff about Mary's personal details. Mary is furious because although she is entitled to these benefits, she would rather other people did not know about her personal circumstances. Mary wants to take out a grievance because Sal has broken the confidentiality code.

▷ What do you think Mary should do first?

Mary should go to her line manager and explain what has happened, and then ask for help in following the grievance procedure. The organisation should be helpful and supportive. They should give guidance and take quick action to resolve the situation. Each of these actions would demonstrate respect and value for Mary, as well as demonstrating organisational responsibility.

Benefits to individuals of avoiding discriminatory practice

Some of these benefits are fairly obvious and have already been covered, but the less obvious ones are discussed overleaf.

GIVE IT A GO   benefits to individvals

Working with another student, make notes as to how anti-discriminatory practice can lead to:

- improved health
- better access to services
- improved standards of living.

Better relationships

••• *External relationships*

Better relationships can work internally and externally. It is clear that if you do not discriminate against an individual, you will get on better with him or her. You will be able to learn all the things the individual has to teach you and you can teach him or her about yourself. In other words, there is a 'mutually beneficial' relationship – you both benefit.

••• *Internal relationships*

When people are unhappy or worried, they often 'take it out' on family members. Have you heard the expression 'you always hurt the one you love'? When people are being discriminated against they are unlikely to be happy and content, and their family relationships may suffer as a consequence. Therefore, living in an anti-discriminatory society will help to bring about better family relationships.

Stronger economy and confident individvals

These two benefits go together because confident individuals are often in control of their lives. They feel good about themselves and are able to contribute positively to society. This means that they can access work and the rewards that come from this (e.g. a salary). In turn, people who are working and spending the money that they earn, help the economy to become stronger, which is something we all benefit from.

▣▣▣ EVIDENCE ACTIVITY

Stereotypical images

Make notes to show one change you would make to your behaviour towards others as a result of the new information you have learned whilst studying this unit. Explain why you want to make the change you have identified.

Index

LEARNING ZONE
DEESIDE COLLEGE